JAPANESE-INSPIRED GARDENS

Adapting Japan's Design Traditions for Your Garden

Patricia Jonas-Guest Editor

Cover: a Japanese-inspired home garden in Brookline,
Massachusetts. Above: a temple garden in Kyoto.

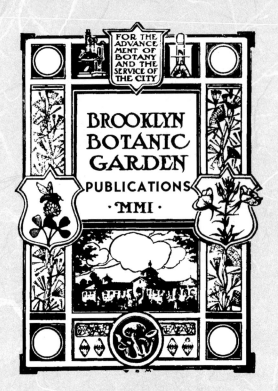

FOR THE ADVANCE MENT OF BOTANY AND THE SERVICE OF THE CITY

BROOKLYN BOTANIC GARDEN PUBLICATIONS · MMI ·

Janet Marinelli
SERIES EDITOR

Sigrun Wolff Saphire
ASSOCIATE EDITOR

Mark Tebbitt
SCIENCE EDITOR

Anne Garland
ART DIRECTOR

Steven Clemants
VICE-PRESIDENT, SCIENCE & PUBLICATIONS

Judith D. Zuk
PRESIDENT

Elizabeth Scholtz
DIRECTOR EMERITUS

Handbook #166
Copyright © Spring 2001 by the Brooklyn Botanic Garden, Inc.
Handbooks in the *21st-Century Gardening Series,* formerly *Plants & Gardens,*
are published quarterly at 1000 Washington Ave., Brooklyn, NY 11225.
Subscription included in Brooklyn Botanic Garden subscriber membership dues ($35.00 per year).
ISSN # 0362-5850   ISBN # 1-889538-20-5
Printed by Science Press, a division of the Mack Printing Group.
Printed on recycled paper.

TABLE OF CONTENTS

INTRODUCTION:
Japanese Inspirations ....Patricia Jonas   4

AUTHENTICITY IN JAPANESE
LANDSCAPE DESIGN ....David Slawson   8

THE GARDEN PATH AS A JOURNEY ....Marc Peter Keane   24

ROCKS IN THE JAPANESE-
INSPIRED GARDEN ....David Harris Engel   34

WATER IN THE JAPANESE
GARDEN STYLE...Judy Glattstein   44

PRUNING TREES AND SHRUBS.........................Douglas M. Roth   54

ENCYCLOPEDIA OF PLANTS FOR
THE JAPANESE-INSPIRED GARDEN....................Patricia Jonas   66
Deep Mountains and Forests   69
Hills and Fields...   78
Ponds and Streams..   84
Seashores   88
Grasses, Sedges, and Bamboos..   93
Ferns and Mosses...   96

USDA Hardiness Zone Map...   99

Suppliers.. 100

For More Information.. 104

Contributors.. 106

Index.. 108

JAPANESE

INSPIRATIONS

PATRICIA JONAS

FOR SEVERAL DECADES, and some would argue for most of the 20th century, American gardeners have been embracing lessons learned from great English, Italian, and French gardens while developing a uniquely American style of gardening. Still, most of us have not been able to figure out what to do with lessons from Japanese gardens, despite the excellent solutions they offer to some very contemporary woes—diminishing space for gardening and loss of everyday contact with the natural world.

Since the last decade of the 19th century, Japanese-style gardens have been a part of the North American landscape. They have been built as exotic displays for World's Fairs and installed in public gardens. They have been built for resorts, restaurants, and miniature golf courses. They have been built on great estates and in suburban yards. They are everywhere, and yet all too often, Japanese-style gardens are merely an overlay of Japanesque elements on the landscape. Very few American gardeners have effectively assimilated the lessons of this magnificent 1400-year-old gardening tradition and built gardens that possess the serenity and perfect harmony of the best Japanese examples (there are hackneyed gardens in Japan, too). In "Authenticity in Japanese Landscape Design," David Slawson suggests we are led away from the essence of a good Japanese garden by depending on the "authenticity" of the materials with which we build, rather than being true to the spirit of Japanese gardening and building with appropriate local materials.

Given a tradition as culturally sophisticated and historically rich as Japanese gardening, we can only begin to elucidate some of its basic principles, aesthetics, and design practices in this short book. We concern ourselves very little with symbolism that may have had significance for 10th-century Japanese aristocrats or 16th-century Japanese monks but has no meaning for us and almost as little for contemporary Japanese. We

In the best Japanese gardens there is evidence of intelligent and active engagement with nature. A beautiful example is the Garden at the Katsura Imperial Villa in Kyoto.

focus instead on elements with universal significance: water, for instance, is associated with cleansing and purification in most cultures, even if it does not possess the powerful sacred qualities it does in Japan.

We hope to inspire you to create gardens using Japanese principles and practices, relying on few, if any, of the stereotypical signs announcing "this is a Japanese garden." If we inadvertently offer formulas here, do not rely on them; instead, take these principles and break new ground. The resulting garden will be authentic in the best sense. On the other hand, if it is the vermilion bridges and stone lanterns you love, incorporate them into your European-style garden as you would gazing globes, gazebos, or any other architectural elements and garden art, classical or whimsical. Read no further unless it is the heart of the Japanese garden you wish to reveal within your garden space.

Certainly not all Japanese gardens are made in the same style, but in every good garden there is evidence of intelligent and active engagement with nature. No other gardening tradition has culminated in a more perfect integration of house, garden, and landscape. The finest example is the Katsura Imperial Villa and Garden in Kyoto, but the same harmony can be found in the smallest tsubo-niwa (courtyard garden). To build a satisfying garden, it is necessary to observe nature closely enough to be able to dis-

Close observation of nature enables the gardener to distill sights, sounds, and fragrances and express them with an absolute economy of means.

till sights, sounds, and fragrances and express them with an absolute economy of means—a simple grouping of rocks, plants, and water. The result must be an elegant balance of opposites: mass and emptiness, light and dark colors, smooth and rough textures, sound and silence, and revealing and hiding.

In "The Garden Path as a Journey," Marc Peter Keane explores his theme in two classic Japanese garden styles, the tea garden and the stroll garden. We learn how techniques like revealing and hiding scenes along a path (mie-gakure) can shape our experience of time and space in the garden, and how the outside world is left behind in stages as one follows the path more deeply into the calm of the garden. In "Rocks in the Japanese-inspired Garden," David Engel offers advice on the best ways to choose and set rock in relation to other rocks, plants, and the ground plane; how to reveal the nature of each; and how to use rock to shape the movement of water and give it a voice. In "Water in the Japanese Garden Style," Judy Glattstein offers practical advice on introducing water regardless of how small your garden space might be. In "Pruning Trees and Shrubs," Douglas Roth demonstrates several key techniques and basic approaches to the all-important art of pruning—revealing the natural character of trees through careful shaping and editing.

We don't pretend to cover every subject and hope readers will develop their connoisseurship by visiting exemplary Japanese-style gardens in the United States and by visiting museums where there is a great deal to

The essence of a natural scene is expressed in this Zen garden at the Mount Tremper Monastery in upstate New York.

learn about garden aesthetics from Japanese painting. Although you will find many practical tips in it, this book is not intended to be a construction manual for the Japanese garden. For instance, it does not include a chapter on building fences and walls. The essential aspect of fences, walls, and hedges is that they provide enclosure in virtually every Japanese garden, defining space and setting the garden apart but not closing it off from the rest of world. If you wish to use a classic design in your garden, consult *Japanese Gardening in Small Spaces* or *A Japanese Touch for your Garden* (see "For More Information," page 104) for some of the hundreds of traditional Japanese patterns for fences and walls.

Choosing and setting plants in the Japanese garden is based on an ancient gardening principle of "natural habitat." We've organized the encyclopedia to demonstrate how to use plants with their natural allies to define ecoregions within the garden. We do not limit our plant choices to natives, but like ancient Japanese garden manuals, we suggest that plants not associated with an ecosystem's vegetation can be dissonant notes in the scene. Instead of piling on plants with horticultural bravado to achieve dramatic visual effects, the Japanese gardener subtracts, to make the garden quiet. Practice reductionism: if you have twenty plants, choose the one that is naturally the dominant plant in each stratum, and use only those few. In a world where garden greed is a virtue and plantoholics are celebrated, this is the radical message of Japanese garden design.

AUTHENTICITY IN JAPANESE LANDSCAPE DESIGN

DAVID SLAWSON

KUO HSI (1020 to 1090 A.D.), one of China's great landscape painters, was an astute observer of how the moods of nature affect the human senses. "The din of the dusty world and the locked-in-ness of human habitations are what human nature habitually abhors," he wrote, "while…mist and the haunting spirits of the mountains are what human nature seeks, and yet can rarely find. How delightful then to have a landscape painted by a skilled hand! Without leaving the room, at once we find ourselves among the streams and ravines…" Japanese garden design, like landscape painting and haiku, developed out of this yearning to experience our essential oneness with nature. For 14 centuries this landscape art has been responding to the beauty of nature and to human culture.

Today, more than a century after being introduced to the West, Japanese gardens are enjoyed throughout the world. But the quality of these gardens and our understanding of what constitutes good design run the gamut from sublime to stereotypical. Are these gardens satisfying the deep yearnings of which Kuo Hsi wrote? Or are they relying on clichés for their appeal? What makes for authenticity in Japanese landscape design?

TWO PATHS TO AUTHENTICITY

There are two quite different paths to authenticity in Japanese gardening. The quickest way to tell them apart is to consider two key aspects of the design process—the sources of inspiration and the choice of materials. The first and most facile of the two approaches is a literal interpretation of

Opposite: The dry landscape garden of Daisen-in translates the effects of Japanese monochrome ink painting into a three-dimensional composition of rocks and plants.

the tradition—the lower path. Here, creative response takes a back seat to precedent: formulas and stereotypes guide the design, rather than the intrinsic nature of the situation and universal design principles. This path to authenticity often results in gardens empty of significance and unintegrated with the landscapes around them. Two obvious examples are "Zen" gardens and the use of stone lantern replicas.

A wealthy Japanese industrialist, in a gesture of friendship for an American city, offered to create an "authentic" Japanese garden. From Japan, he sent 500 orchid trees, a 300-year-old lantern, six additional stone lanterns, an eight-ton, eight-foot-high granite statue of Hotei (the smiling god of prosperity), a 15-foot-tall stone pagoda, three bridges, a teahouse, and an arbor. He also hired a famous Japanese landscape architect, six Japanese carpenters, and three Japanese gardeners. Yet the resulting landscape was burdened by clichés and lacked the sublimity we immediately recognize in the best Japanese gardens.

On the precedent-driven path to authenticity, the authority for the design comes from the outside and is imposed—upon those who will use the garden, upon the site (a certain amount of adaptation to the site is acceptable as long as it does not violate precedent), and upon the choice and use of materials (if the "right" types of rocks, ornaments such as stone lanterns, and plants are not available locally, they are imported. Indeed, importing them from Japan makes them more authentic).

The second, higher, path to authenticity follows a metaphorical, situation-driven approach to the tradition. Here, the inspiration for the design comes from within—from the desires and culture of those who will use the garden, from the site and its surroundings (including the regional landscape), and from locally available materials. While those with a shallow understanding of tradition tend to adhere more rigidly to convention, those with a deeper understanding are free to respond to the situation and, in so doing, break with precedent. My teacher, Kinsaku Nakane, put it this way: "Japanese garden design is totally free." David Engel, who apprenticed under Tansai Sano in Kyoto in the 1950s, recalls his teacher's frequent insistence that "I feel free when designing gardens. 'Don't be held down by tired, outworn ideas and practices,' he would say."

Examples abound of Japanese garden designs that broke with precedent in inspired responses to specific situations. The dry landscape garden (karesansui) of Daisen-in was created during the same era when Japanese monochrome ink painting emulating the Chinese masters of the Sung period reached its peak in Japan, the late 15th and early 16th century. The garden translates the atmospheric effects of this style of painting into a three-dimensional composition of rocks and plants, almost as if the landscape had been painted on the outer walls of this Zen Buddhist temple. The craggy peaks, set against the white plaster wall (which serves much

This dry landscape garden with brook in Colorado evokes the surrounding landscape—the technique at the heart of Japanese garden design.

the same function as white paper or silk), seem shrouded in mist. Gardens like Daisen-in and the now-famous garden at Ryoan-ji are prototypes—inspired responses to their cultural environment that lend fresh new voices to the tradition of landscape evocation.

Necessity is the mother of invention, as the adage goes, and played an important part in the evolution of another Japanese garden prototype, the tea garden. This new landscape form sought to re-create the experience of imbibing a cup of green tea in the ambiance of a rustic hermit's hut. In *Space and Illusion in the Japanese Garden*, Teiji Itoh tells the story of a 15th-century shogun, Ashikaga Yoshimasa, who, returning one day from a hawking expedition, stopped at a tea master's hermitage. Because the path through the garden was muddy, Yoshimasa's attendants spread out things for him to walk on. As the story goes, this gave the tea master the idea of laying flat stones at intervals along the garden path. So it appears that stepping stones were at first used as a practical solution.

Half a century later, the great tea master Sen no Rikyu (1521–1591) asserted that stepping stones were 60 percent functional and 40 percent aesthetic. By the early 17th century, Rikyu's distinguished disciple, Furuta Oribe (1544–1615), had reversed his teacher's formula, and a tea garden without stepping stones was unthinkable. In a still later development, the

Left and opposite: Two free interpretations of the stone water basin, one of the most familiar elements of the tea garden.

courtyard garden, a style developed for the space between the outer shop and inner living quarters of Kyoto's urban commoners, stepping stones were used purely for their aesthetic appeal; they had no practical function.

Prototypes become types and, finally, stereotypes. By the time Englishman Josiah Conder went to Japan in the 1870s to teach Western architecture at the Imperial University of Tokyo, the gardens he saw were clichés. His *Landscape Architecture in Japan* (1893) was the first detailed book on Japanese gardens available to Westerners. "In spite of his really great efforts to learn about gardens, Conder's knowledge of his subject was extremely limited," asserts Loraine Kuck in *The World of the Japanese Garden,* "for it was derived almost entirely from the decadent [late] Tokugawa [and early Meiji] gardens in Tokyo" and from the popular how-to books of the time. "The pictures and his report on the curiously poetic names for rocks and trees and the astounding conventions said to rule the garden craft of Japan," she wrote, "aroused interest in Japanese gardens which has never abated. It also led to considerable misunderstanding." Unfortunately, such misconceptions continue to mislead many today.

A gardener at one public Japanese garden once confided to me, with some chagrin, that at a committee meeting some members had expressed the desire to "enhance" the garden by adding black rope and wood crutch supports to the pine trees, something they apparently had seen in other Japanese gardens. The problem, of course, is that they

were fascinated by the trappings but did not reflect on their purpose. Fortunately, other committee members rejected the idea, comparing black rope and crutch supports for the pines to a perfectly healthy person walking around with bandages and a cane. In fact, this technique of using black rope and wooden crutches to support or alter the position of tree branches is rarely needed, and rarely used, in Japan. My apprenticeship taught me that the primary technique for guiding the growth of trees is selective pruning, done throughout the life and according to the growth habit of the specimen.

No Japanese garden motif has been governed by more formulaic rules, or more freely interpreted, than another tea garden element, the stone water basin. Usually set on the ground so that one must crouch down to dip the water, the basin evokes a mountain brook flowing into a pool of cool, pure water where one can rinse away the cares of the world and refresh the spirit. There are basins with natural shapes, basins hollowed out of recycled foundation stones, and others with geometrical designs. Northeast of the Shokintei teahouse at the Katsura Villa in Kyoto, stepping stones lead down to the rocky shore and out into the pond, where guests can rinse their hands. Here, the water basin archetype has been expanded to embrace the shores of a pond, an idea attributed to famed garden designer Kobori Enshu (1579–1647). This is the kind of metaphorical leap that occurs when a designer is sensitive not

only to the demands of tradition but also to the possibilities of the site and the client's taste. Enshu manages to evoke a mountain hut perched on a rocky shore and at the same time remind us of the origin of the water basin—a crystal stream where people, as well as other creatures, would come for cleansing and refreshment.

Why not take our cues from such examples? Why not tailor ornaments like stone lanterns and water basins out of local materials to meet the needs of the individual garden and make it the *exception* to use imported designs? A recycled old barn stone might serve as a "lighthouse" on a desolate shore, or native stones might be used to create a stone lantern. A water basin might be a hollowed-out glacial granite boulder, or cast-in-place concrete with the aggregate exposed by washing before it fully sets up. The water basin spout, if there is one, might be made of black bamboo, if it happens to be growing locally, or from the branch of a sycamore tree.

Samuel Newsom offers a useful guideline for incorporating stone ornaments in Japanese landscape design. "People are sometimes carried away by an object because it is old or has a history, regardless of its suitability and artistic value," he observes in *Japanese Garden Construction*. He encourages readers to resist that tendency and include in their garden designs "only necessary things, or things which truly contribute to the beauty of the scene."

Opposite and right: Two examples of Japanese-inspired gardens created in North America. Both take inspiration from native landscapes and do not rely on lanterns or other stereotypical elements for authenticity.

GENERAL DESIGN GUIDELINES

Design the garden so that its beauty accords with the site and responds to the passage of time as sensitively as do leaves in a whispering breeze, with nothing clumsy or coarse about it. The result must be fascinating in a quiet, graceful way.

The above passage from *Illustrations for Designing Mountain, Water, and Hillside Field Landscapes* (1466), sets a high standard for landscape designers, one that cannot be achieved simply by following rules. Even the author of *Tsukiyama Teizoden* (1828), the first "do-it-yourself" Japanese garden manual, cautioned against taking the rules he set down too seriously: "Though these are called rules, they are simply intended to show the general principles to which people should adhere. These laws are not fixed and immutable. A stone by such and such a name need not be placed here and another there unless desired. They are only suggestions to be developed appropriately. People fettered by formal ideas should realize this and strive to improve their art." Josiah Conder, if he was aware of it, did not transmit this caution to his Western audience.

If rules are too rigid, then what sort of principles might better guide us when we create Japanese gardens? If we think metaphorically, we can find some general guidelines applicable to a wide range of design situations, and avoid getting bogged down by formulas and details.

I found my own bare-bones framework for responding to design situations in the theory of landscape design implicit in the opening two pages of the *Illustrations.* The gist of this theory is that a good garden results when the designer is attuned to three essential sources of information and inspiration: the needs and desires of the persons for whom the garden is being created, the nature of the site and the surrounding landscape, and the nature of locally available materials. It's handy to have a name for this triad of essential sources of information and inspiration, so I call it the "Accord Triangle."

Some things to consider about the user's nature and needs are: what is his or her favorite landscape? What is the budget? More universal design strategies come into play here as well, such as making the garden pleasing to the senses, and making it resonate with its cultural context. Site considerations include topography, solar orientation, prevailing winds, and any existing trees and architectural elements. The nature of the site and surrounding landscape are important sources of inspiration for the garden design. For example, a wooded hillside might suggest a path leading to a small viewing pavilion. Rocks and plants are locally, or at least regionally, available materials that can inspire the design. Are the rocks, which are used to create geological effects, smooth or craggy or in flat slabs? Is the soil rocky, sandy, or clay loam? Is it poorly or well drained? Is the site sunny or shady? Such factors will determine which plants will best evoke the desired landscape experience.

The nature of the site and the surrounding landscape served as important sources of inspiration for this Colorado garden, with its potentilla meadow.

This approach to creating a Japanese garden is driven by both the specific situation and universal principles of human perception. It makes us responsive to the range of feelings, forces, and qualities that manifest themselves in each unique design situation, rather than forcing us to adhere to a limited range of acceptable forms prescribed by an external authority. It is a way of working from the inside out, as opposed to superimposing an external style or set of ideas. It also encourages us, as we are urged by the author of the *Illustrations*, to "maintain an attitude of reverence and respect, ...and not simply do what [we] alone find interesting." Neither the garden designer nor the viewer is a blank slate; rather, each of us is a reservoir of past experience. The Japanese garden tradition opens our eyes not only to the beauty of the landscape of our own country and region, but also to its reflection in our own cultural heritage and personal experience.

TIMELESS DESIGN PRINCIPLES

An intuitive awareness of timeless principles—universal truths of nature, including human nature—enables us to effectively design the garden in accord with both the natural environment and the human body. The timeless truths of nature are built into the very fiber of our being; we need no formal learning to apprehend them. We all grasp intuitively the "meaning" of a mountain torrent rushing through its rocky chasm; of a meandering river, wide in the foreground and narrowing to a thread in the distance; or of an ancient gnarled tree, with snaking roots anchoring it in the rock and a thick, twisting trunk spiraling out in a dance of windswept branches.

PROPORTION

Registering on our senses directly, proportional relationships have the power to evoke such aesthetic feelings as movement, depth, harmony, and serenity. Certain ratios occur frequently in nature and exert a special pull on our senses. The Golden Section (1:1.618) is the supreme example: it occurs in nature in everything from coiled fern fronds to sea shells and has been applied in the arts of cultures as different as those of Japan and Greece. One does not have to look far in Japanese gardens to discover the use of this proportion. For example, the 15th-century garden manual, the *Illustrations*, specifies how different-size rocks relate to one another in landscape compositions; by far the most common proportion is the Golden Section. It is clear in the *Illustrations*, however, that such proportions should not be taken as absolutes, but rather as guides, to be interpreted according to the situation, through the designer's intuition.

Thinking in terms of horizontal, vertical, and diagonal planes helps structure a garden design. As in the rock formation above, the diagonal plane evokes exciting dynamism.

THE HORIZONTAL, VERTICAL AND DIAGONAL PLANES

Working closely with proportion are the "Three Forces" (also described in the *Illustrations*)—horizontal, vertical, and diagonal. The Three Forces are powerful tools for structuring our designs, as each one can be counted upon to elicit a specific and fundamental aesthetic response. The horizontal plane, associated with level earth and bodies of water, evokes an expansive, easy movement, and thus serenity. The vertical plane evokes the tension and power required when movement is heavenward, in opposition to the force of gravity. In the garden, or nature, this is felt in towering rock formations, and the threadlike waterfalls that sometimes plummet from such precipices. Daisen-in's twin peaks, like Manhattan's early skyscrapers and Gothic cathedrals, use diminishing proportion (they progressively narrow toward the top) to heighten their verticality. The diagonal plane, associated with such vertical objects as trees succumbing to the force of gravity and upthrust rock formations, evokes an exciting dynamism bordering on instability. Together, the Three Forces form the three sides of a scalene triangle, a triangle with unequal sides. An asymmetry of forces always feels more natural, dynamic, and inviting in the garden, just as it does in the natural landscape.

Partially concealed, an S-curve path invites further exploration and enhances the sense of mystery and depth in Japanese gardens.

THE S-CURVE AND Z-ZIGZAG

To the Three Forces, we need to add one other essential element that enlivens both Japanese gardens and natural landscape with its well-proportioned twists and turns—the S-curve. A softening of the Z-zigzag, the S-curve is evident in the flow of rivers and highways, as well as in the lines that define the edge between land and sea, foothills and prairie, or hills and valley. While the sharp-cornered Z-zigzag may be used to evoke rocky mountain landscapes, the S-curve is found in more gentle terrain, where the topography has eroded over the ages.

The S-curve is also one of a number of techniques used to enhance the sense of mystery and depth in Japanese gardens. An S-curve path, for example, invites further exploration and is universally preferred over a straight path, which reveals all at a glance. The sense of mystery can be deepened with techniques of "hide-and-reveal" (mie-gakure) by obscuring the path here and there with plantings, rock outcroppings, or hillocks in a natural way.

The partially concealed S-curve works its magic in the vertical plane as well as the horizontal ground plane. In nature, and in Japanese gardens, we find it in the sculptural trunk and branching of evergreens like pines and junipers, with their green-tufted foliage floating in cloudlike layers.

Stepping stones once served a practical function, allowing visitors to walk a muddy path without getting their feet wet, but now are often used for purely aesthetic reasons.

The Chinese and Japanese for centuries have used pruning techniques that simulate the effects of wind and age: an umbrella-shaped crown, an S-curved trunk, and a zigzag branching structure revealed in the spaces between masses of foliage at the branch tips. A visceral sense of rootedness, of connection to the earth, is evoked by the thick, gnarled trunk and outstretching branches of the tree's lower portion, while an ethereal sense, the visual equivalent of the sound of wind soughing through pines, is evoked by the airy filigree of upper branches silhouetted against the sky.

We need not be limited to pines or even conifers to achieve such effects. We can choose other trees that appeal to us from our own environment and experience. A similar gnarled branching pattern and proportionate decreasing of branch spacing is characteristic of such North American natives as sassafras and persimmon, for instance. It is very much in the spirit of Japanese design to look to locally available materials, rather than exotics, to satisfy our design needs.

EVOCATION OF NATURAL SCENERY

Evocation of natural scenery is at the heart of Japanese landscape design. This is emphasized in the general guidelines at the beginning of the 11th century manual, *Sakuteiki* (*Notes on Garden Making*):

> You should design each part of the garden tastefully, recalling your memories of how nature presented itself for each feature...Think

Enhancing awareness of natural beauty and translating the essence of this experience for the garden is one of the great accomplishments of Japanese design.

over the famous places of scenic beauty throughout the land, and...design your garden with the mood of harmony, modeling after the general air of such places.

While *Sakuteiki's* author could not have imagined that his words would be read by foreigners eight centuries after he wrote them, he would have understood our fervent desire to grasp the underlying spirit and principles of this landscape art. Were he to travel to North America and other foreign lands today, I think he would be the first to recommend that we take the metaphorical path to authenticity—that is, take inspiration from our own native landscapes.

When Kinsaku Nakane designed Tenshin-en, the Japanese dry landscape garden at the Boston Museum of Fine Arts, he found inspiration not in the scenic landscapes of Japan but rather, as he put it, in New England's "rocky coastlines, deep forests, soft hillsides, and craggy mountains." A composition of 150 boulders brought from Boston's North Shore and set into undulating earth mounds evokes the geological structure of nearby mountains and offshore islands. Plants like Japanese cryptomeria, stewartia, and maple are combined with Eastern hemlock and American holly to evoke the natural habitat of a New England mixed hardwood-conifer forest. Native conifers with lighter green needles, such as tamarack or white spruce, could easily have taken the place of cryptomeria to serve as a contrast with the darker green hemlock. And native small trees like amelanchier or mountain maple could have served as well as Japanese maples and stewartia to evoke the hardwoods. Using native

For centuries, garden designers in Japan have found inspiration in such coastal scenery as that along the Japan Sea.

plants is very much in the spirit of Japanese garden aesthetics, and planting so as to re-create the essence of natural habitats is a basic principle of Japanese garden design set forth in the *Illustrations*. Which habitats one chooses to evoke will, of course, depend on the site and design inspiration. The beauty of Japanese garden design is in large part due to integration—things are done because they are fitting rather than for show. This larger principle underlies the higher path of authenticity and is aptly illustrated by an exchange between between tea master Sen no Rikyu and a pupil as related in *Cha-no-Yu: The Japanese Tea Ceremony:*

> Seto Kamon Masatada of Omi was first a retainer of the house of Hojo and afterwards served Toyotomi Hideyoshi. He was Rikyu's pupil in Tea and became so expert that he was numbered among the Seven Masters of the day. He was once invited to Rikyu's house and after the tea was over he happened to notice a dipper that lay on the shelf and was much taken with its shape, praising it exceedingly.
>
> Rikyu asked what he saw in it, and he replied that it looked a better shape than those commonly used. "Indeed," said Rikyu, "and why?" "It seems to be a bit shorter than usual, and that gives it a very interesting appearance," replied Masatada. "I should like to have one like it." Some time after this Masatada invited Rikyu to his

Garden designers in America should follow the example of great Japanese designers and turn to local scenery for inspiration, such as Wyoming's Teton Mountains, above.

house, and when the tea was over and the utensils were being put away, Rikyu remarked, "The dipper you used today seems a bit too short." "Ah, but I liked the look of the one I saw at your house so well that I made my own short to match it," replied Masatada. "Ah," said Rikyu with a sigh, "I am afraid you don't yet understand the real spirit of tea, though I thought you did. I am a little man, as you see, and so I have a small dipper to suit my size. But you, on the other hand, are a big fellow, so it is natural for you to use a larger one. What do you want with a small one?" At this enlightenment dawned suddenly on Masatada, and in the future he had a large size dipper made.

Sometimes we need encouragement to move from focusing narrowly and literally to seeing the larger picture—to move from the low to the high path of authenticity. Japanese garden design is not just a style of landscaping. It is an art deeply rooted in a way of thinking and feeling about our place in nature. To me, one of the wonders of the art of the Japanese garden is that it has shown a great capacity for seamlessly merging evolving human knowledge with the wisdom of wildness. For this reason it can serve as a beacon to human cultures in the coming centuries, as we seek ways to live in harmony with our earthly home.

THE GARDEN PATH AS A JOURNEY

MARC PETER KEANE

INSIDE A MOSSY, ROOFED GATE, half hidden by luxuriant foliage, a garden path beckons. Tempted, you enter, and in doing so, begin a journey. The garden path as a journey—an unusual idea perhaps? Nowhere is it more true than in the tea gardens and stroll gardens of Japan, though for very different reasons—the former being a journey of spirit and aesthetics, and the latter, one of time and space. Understanding how the path has been given meaning in these garden forms not only allows a deeper appreciation of Japanese gardens, but also yields abundant ideas for designers who wish to incorporate aspects of Japanese gardens in their own landscapes.

THE TEA GARDEN: A JOURNEY OF SPIRIT AND AESTHETICS

Tea gardens developed during Japan's medieval period, first appearing in the early 17th century along with the advent of the tea ceremony itself, more properly known as chanoyu or sado, the Way of Tea. In order to achieve the appropriate quietude of spirit required to appreciate the aesthetics of sado, a place of preparation was required, and the development of that space marked the beginning of the tea garden. Ideally, this preparatory ground captures the sensory experience of a trip away from busy town life to a secluded mountain hut, passing through forested hills along the way.

To evoke the sense of a long journey in the small space between garden entry and teahouse, these gardens employ a series of thresholds, each one accentuating the feeling of passage, of entering progressively deeper into a new world. The thresholds begin with a roofed outer gate, sotomon, which separates the tea garden from the outside world. After entering, the last guest turns to the gate and closes the wooden doors, shutting them with a wooden cross-bolt. The dull smite of wood on wood signals the arrival of guests to the host, who waits unseen inside. To those

To evoke the sense of a long journey in the small space between garden entry and tea-house, tea gardens employ a series of thresholds, each one accentuating the feeling of passage, of entering progressively deeper into a new world.

who have just entered, it has a deeper meaning: they are no longer part of the world they just left. The dual concepts of a tea garden as a place of passage and as a purified place separate from the outer world are also reflected in the common name for the tea garden, roji. One meaning of roji is "alleyway," which implies passage; but the word is also found in the *Lotus Sutra*, in which there is an allegory comparing the profane world to a burning house and the pure world to a roji (outer world), to which the enlightened may escape from the flames.

Continuing through the tea garden, guests walk slowly along a path through the garden. If there are several paths, then those not to be used are marked as being closed by placing a single round river stone tied with a black palm-fiber cord on a stepping stone in the path; a simple symbol that means "do not enter."

Finding a small, roofed waiting bench, called a koshikake machiai, guests sit down and wait quietly for their host to invite them forward. There is no compelling reason to make them wait; preparations for the tea gathering were most likely begun at dawn (when water drawn from the well is most cool and fresh) and have been complete for some time. No, the guests are allowed to wait, giving them time to commune with the

ephemeral qualities of the garden: crickets chirping, dew on moss, wind rustling in the trees.

The next threshold in the garden is a small gate, called a middle gate, chumon, that stands halfway between the outer entry and the teahouse itself. The portion of the garden first entered from the outer gate is known as the outer garden, soto roji, while the portion nearer the teahouse is the inner garden, uchi roji; the middle gate marks the separation between the two. Although some are beautifully detailed roofed gates, more often than not a middle gate is a simple panel of loosely woven split bamboo attached to an upright post, its significance being not in its elaborate design but simply in its presence.

Having passed the middle gate, guests stop next at a water laver, tsukubai, where they rinse their hands and mouths in a ritual act of cleansing, a preparation of body and spirit prerequisite to entering the teahouse. The laver is usually a stone that has been carved with a basin to hold water and is set low to the ground—thus the name tsukubai, which derives from the verb tsukubau, to crouch down. The low position of the laver requires that those who use it bow down before it; the lowering of the body before water is an intentional act, showing humility before the "wellspring of life." Cleansing complete, the guests move forward in single file to the entry of the teahouse, nijiriguchi, a square door so small that they are forced to bow down in order to pass. This is another act of humility, in this case intended to express that all those who enter to join the gathering are equal.

Gates to be entered; benches for quiet communing; water to cleanse; a series of thresholds in the garden, some physical, some inward—by passing through the garden, the guests are changed, calmed, and made more aware of subtleties, all in preparation for the tea gathering that follows.

Opposite: Halfway between entrance and teahouse visitors passing through the garden approach a second threshold called the middle gate.
Right: A stone tied with rope signals that a path is not to be used.

The tea garden is not a "garden" at all, in the sense of a place to gather and display plants or prized stones. It is not meant to be stunningly attractive, nor to impress visitors with a splendid horticultural display. Rather, it is given over primarily to broadleaf and coniferous evergreen trees and shrubs, and contains few, if any, flowering plants; the change of the seasons is noted in more subtle ways. The tea garden is simply a path, and the path itself a journey.

In order to recreate a tea garden on your own property, it is not necessary to mimic the precise forms that exist in Japan, nor to use the same materials that are employed there. The most important thing is to grasp the essence of a tea garden and creatively reconstruct that in your garden. The tea garden is a path that evokes a spiritual or aesthetic change in those who pass along it. In Japan, tea gardens are designed to instill the aesthetics of reserve and rusticity, known as wabi or sabi, in preparation for partaking of matcha (whisked tea); however, the path you design for yourself could have a different intent. The essential aspects that must be included are the sense of passage from "one place" to "another," and a sense of calm. The former is best accomplished by creating a series of thresholds in the garden that lend a feeling of depth and passage as one moves through them. The sense of calm is best achieved by designing with an understated naturalness and a rarefied palette.

THE STROLL GARDEN:
A JOURNEY OF TIME AND SPACE

Another type of Japanese garden that places great importance on the path is the stroll garden. Stroll gardens usually are quite large and have a pond in the central area encircled by a path (or several paths), which allows visitors to stroll about. These gardens developed after the medieval period, from the 17th to 19th centuries, when travel throughout the country was severely limited by the central government. Because the lords couldn't travel freely, they created private gardens where such "excursions" could be undertaken. In their gardens they built a number of scenes that reminded visitors of famous places from around the country, familiar from well-known tales and woodblock prints, as well as from stories told by those returning from religious pilgrimages (one of the few kinds of travel for which it was possible to obtain a permit). By traveling about the garden path, visitors could take "excursions" designed for them by their host.

Among the famous scenes depicted in stroll gardens were natural landscapes such as Mount Fuji, Amanohashidate (a famous spot along the Japan Sea coast), and the Oi River near Kyoto. The scenes also included built objects such as Togetsukyo and Tsutenkyo, both famous bridges near Kyoto. One garden owner even went so far as to have an entire postal

Stroll gardens usually feature a pond surrounded by a path. Along the path a series of scenes develops, transporting the visitor to faraway places.

town reconstructed for the pleasure of his guests, who may not have had a chance to see such an "exotic" out-of-the-way place. Some scenes were reminiscent not of Japan but of China, like the Su dike in the West Lake near Hangzhou; and other gardens contained scenes that were drawn from poetry rather than actual localities, often poetry of the earlier, Heian period. The path that meandered about the garden passed these various scenes, hiding and revealing them in turns (a technique called mie-gakure), allowing the visitor to take a broad excursion within the confines of the garden.

The scenes were not recreated in miniature, as in a model, but rather were expressed symbolically. The essence of a natural scene was extracted and re-created in the garden. For instance, to evoke the feeling of Amanohashidate, which is a narrow, pine-covered spit of land arcing across a wide bay, all that was needed was one pine tree planted on a short peninsula in a pond, edged with some well-placed boulders.

The paths of the stroll gardens, like those of the tea gardens, elicit the sense of embarking on a journey. Unlike the tea garden, however, the journey is not an inward one, but rather one that transcends time and space to allow those who circumambulate the garden to venture to faraway places in times past or present.

If you own a large property and are interested in creating a stroll garden, the key aspect of the design is to develop a series of scenes along a path that meanders around a central element, usually a pond or lake. The scenes may depict whatever you wish. For instance, they could be reflections of the natural world in your area. Such a garden would include a series of "mini-ecosystems," each of which mirrors the geology and flora of the natural environment surrounding your home. This is similar to the aspect of Japanese stroll gardens, which have "mountain, meadow, and ocean" districts within them. The key to designing this way is to not be too literal but rather, as stated in the 11th-century gardening manual, *Sakuteiki*, to "visualize the famous landscapes of our country and come to understand their most interesting points. Re-create the essence of those scenes in the garden but do so interpretatively not strictly."

Another, perhaps more poetic, option for designing a stroll garden is to create scenes that are interpretations not of the physical world, but rather of cultural themes. This is accomplished by creating physical scenes that are in fact contemplative musings on cultural subjects: science, literature, history, and so on. Rikugien, for example, a large stroll garden in Tokyo, employs the six classic themes of poetry as its motif, laying out a series of 88 scenes derived from poetic epithets and themes that were favored by the owner.

DESIGNING PATHS

The speed and cadence of movement through a garden, whether a tea garden or a large stroll garden (or any other garden, for that matter) is determined by the design of the path. Of course, the placement of the path within the garden is important in determining how a garden will be revealed, but it is not the only factor; the design of the path surface itself also influences the experience.

MATERIALS

Imagine yourself on a path made of a material that is easily walked upon, such as smooth gravel or neatly arranged cut granite pavers. You can walk freely, at whatever speed you desire, head held up,

The design of the path determines speed and cadence of movement in the garden.

and look around as you move through the garden. If, however, the path is made of small stepping stones that provide uncertain footing, the speed at which you can walk will drop dramatically, and your movements will become staccato as you navigate from stone to stone. In order to watch your footing, your head will drop, and you will not look around while walking. The way in which your head is held—and thus the way in which the garden is revealed as you pass through—is determined not only by where the path is placed but also by the materials from which it is made.

The designers of tea gardens made maximum use of this technique, creating paths that carefully guide guests through the garden in stages. Modern garden makers can learn much from these master designers of the past: a path made of small stepping stones, for instance, could lead into the garden from the outer gate, then turn into a nobedan, a section of path made of small stones fitted together into a neat rectangular form, somewhat like a rectangular tatami mat (in fact it is also called an ishidatami or stone tatami). Whereas stepping stones are difficult to walk on (forcing the cadence to slow and the head to drop), a nobedan is easier to navigate, enabling you to raise your head and look forward. Consequently, it is appropriate to place a nobedan at a point where the sudden lifting of the head will reveal some aspect of the garden—a distant tea-

On a smooth path, you can walk freely and look around the garden.

When the footing is uncertain, you must walk slowly and look down.

Japanese gardens favor asymmetry. Paths tend to meander or develop in a series of straight sections that meet obliquely.

house, a lantern, or some other view. In another design, a stepping stone path could be punctuated by a larger stone, like a garanseki, a round foundation stone that was used as a pedestal for the massive wooden columns in old temples. Whereas you will look down while crossing the stepping stones, once you step up onto the larger stone, you can pause and look about the garden freely. These "punctuation" stones are often placed at a juncture where several paths meet, acting as nodes in the flow of movement through the garden.

The material of which a path is made controls movements and vision, but it also adds the dimension of sound to the garden. Soil paths dampen the sounds of footsteps, gravel adds a crunching sound (with rounded pebbles being more pleasant than crushed gravel) and stepping stones provide a percussive tapping sound. These sounds are heightened when visitors wear wooden sandals; the rubber-soled shoes popular today lessen the intensity of footfall sounds.

BALANCE

Visual balance is another important aspect of path design. Balance in Japanese gardens (as in all of the arts of Japan) can be described as asymmetric and dynamic. Whereas objects of importance in European gardens, such as fountains and sculptures, are typically placed on center with a path, thereby developing the

The material of which a path is made adds the dimension of sound to a garden. Soil paths dampen the sounds of footsteps, while gravel adds a crunching sound.

axial site-line of an allée, Japanese gardens favor asymmetry. When paths are designed asymmetrically, the line they form in the garden tends to meander or, alternatively, develops in a complex series of straight sections that meet each other obliquely. The paths never (or rarely) align "on-center" with an object of importance, a teahouse, lantern, or prominent planting, as in formal European gardens, but rather approach them from an angle, offering oblique views that are less formal.

Those designing Japanese gardens outside of Japan often are tempted to resort to stereotypical elements—raked white sand, red bridges, and so on. But there are other, more subtle ways of designing gardens that may not necessarily contain obvious Japanesque elements, yet still provide the essence of the original. Consider, for instance, the way paths have been used in Japanese gardens—to lead those who walk them on spiritual and spatial journeys—and thoughtfully employ this design principle in your own garden. Having done so, the feeling of a Japanese garden will be transmitted without resorting to stereotypes. After all, we turn to the garden for refreshment, for repose, and for discovery. When a garden path takes us on one of those journeys, it has offered us all it can.

ROCKS IN THE JAPANESE- INSPIRED GARDEN

DAVID HARRIS ENGEL

WHEN PLACED IN EVOCATIVE ARRANGEMENTS in the garden, rocks are reminders of the beauty of pristine natural scenery. In the history of gardening, some of the most notable examples of the use of rocks are found in the karesansui gardens of Japan's Zen temples, which conjure up visions of scenery far beyond their walls. In confined spaces, the makers of these gardens created stunning landscapes composed mainly of stones set in an off-white "sea" of raked gravel, complemented by sparse plantings of bamboo, low-growing trees, shrubs, or patches of moss. The Zen temple garden is as clear an expression of Zen art as Japan's powerful monochromatic ink paintings, and at the same time it is the symbolic expression of an idealized configuration of nature. In its most abstract sense it is also a metaphor for the cosmos, kindling awareness of the large in the small, perceiving an unbounded universe in nature's tiniest and humblest creations—a flower, a bird, an insect, or a stone.

In Japan, an awareness of the suggestive power of rocks, heightened from the earliest times by a perception of their sanctity—they were believed to be the abodes of benevolent spirits—inspired their introduction into gardens. The numinous character attributed to rocks was also attributed to legendary icons, such as Horai, the mystical Chinese island of eternal youth; to creatures of good omen, like the turtle and the crane; and to the auspicious number series seven-five-three, denoting the lucky years in a child's life.

Seeming to grow up from the garden soil yet firmly rooted in place, rocks represent to the Japanese stability and durability in a world that is transitory. The Buddhist consciousness of the transience of life intensifies the desire for a sanctuary that includes familiar, enduring, and consoling elements. Rocks provide this sense of both solidity and reliability but also the sense of the passage of time, signaled by their slow accretions of lichens and the weathering of their surfaces. A single eroded rock can evoke the realms of time and space in the garden.

Rocks not only play a symbolic role but also have many practical uses in the naturalistic gardens of Japan. Boulders and large rocks, for instance, can work as a freestanding wall to screen out undesirable views, and prevent the outside world from intruding on the garden experience. They also can function as a protective fence to restrain children and pets, or simply as a neutral background for other garden elements. You can set rocks into an embankment on a hillside to retain a slope or a terrace. Placed along a streambank, they can prevent erosion as the water careens around the twists and turns of its channel. You can also use rocks to mark a change in the direction of a path, and along garden steps and ramps, preventing soil from spilling onto the steps and pavement.

Natural rocks and worked stone are often used in pavements and bridges, while uncut rocks with at least one flat face are used as tobi-ishi (stepping stones).

Stone artifacts, such as water basins, stone lanterns, and religious sculpture, play secondary roles and should be used sparingly.

Between the utilitarian use of rocks and their purely symbolic role, there is a middle ground in which they play no physically indispensable

Through the weathering of their surfaces and the slow accretion of lichens, rocks provide a sense of the passage of time.

role but do nurture the sense of an aesthetically balanced composition pleasing to the eye. To achieve this effect, study rocks in their natural state, and place them in the garden to look as if natural forces had set them there. The goal is to create a "naturalistic" landscape, perhaps one that evokes distant vistas, demanding no symbolic imagination. The emphasis is on creating a garden with the character of natural scenery, which ironically might necessitate drastically altering the character of the existing landscape.

CREATING NATURALISTIC LANDSCAPE FEATURES

Rocks can enhance a naturalistic garden in many ways. You can use them around featureless shorelines of ponds and streams to create promontories, peninsulas, and islands. You can use rocks to form hilly or mountainous landscapes. (Some grading of level land also may be necessary.) Representations of rugged mountain peaks and crags require sharp, angular, blocky specimens, while smaller, more rounded and smoother rocks suggest the gentle, rolling terrain of an ancient, timeworn landscape.

As you can see, it is important to decide what functions or aesthetic goals the rocks are intended to achieve before you select individual specimens: are they to work as a retaining wall or to be laid flat as stepping stones? Will they be placed along the banks of a rushing mountain brook

Opposite: A rock set in a pond can give the impression of a rocky island emerging from the sea. Right: This rugged composition evokes a waterfall in mountainous terrain in a small space.

or along a slow, meandering stream? Will they be located along the shoreline of a pond or lake? You should also decide, before selecting the actual rocks, what type of natural scenery you would like to evoke—a rugged mountain vista with a lofty waterfall, a series of undulating gentle hills, or a sandy or gravelly beach or a rocky island emerging from the sea? The down-to-earth and mostly simple shapes and textures of the rocks in a Japanese garden (as contrasted with the pierced and convoluted calcareous limestones of Chinese gardens) are mainly achieved with granites—igneous rocks that over eons have metamorphosed into robust stone. Through the choice of the sizes, shapes, and number of rocks in your garden, you have the power to evoke a range of moods and recall to mind a particular kind of landscape.

COMPOSING WITH ROCKS

It's impossible to decide in advance the exact order in which rocks will be placed. Set one rock at a time, then step back to assess the work. As you go along, you need to determine for each rock which sides are the top and the face—that is, which side is up and which is to be seen from the principal viewing point. Think about which facet has the form, surface tex-

When combining rocks, strive for harmony of color and texture.

ture, striations, indentations, and ridges that will evoke most vividly the particular effect you have in mind, be it a rugged mountain peak, a mountain range, or a gentle, rolling hill. Consider each rock's height, surfaces, convexities, and concavities when determining how it will work best in a grouping. To achieve a unified composition, make sure that at least one rock dominates within a grouping. Strive for harmony of color and texture within the grouping *and* with other nearby rocks. It would disrupt harmony, for instance, if you added white quartzite or pale limestone to a composition of dark gray, weathered granite. Bear in mind that the color and size of rocks will also influence perspective. To create the illusion of greater depth and distance, place lighter-colored, larger rocks in the foreground, close to the main viewing point, and darker-colored, smaller rocks in the background, where they will appear to recede. If your budget necessitates the use of artificial rocks, place them in the background as well, as far as possible from the viewer; one natural rock, properly placed, is better than three artificial ones. Avoid concentrating solely on the front view of a rock grouping that will be seen from more than one viewpoint. Instead, arrange the rocks as a three-dimensional composition with evocative views on all sides.

Naturally, you will need some equipment for moving larger rocks. Heavy boulders typically are set using a crane, front-end loader, or back-hoe.

Rocks can play many utilitarian roles, retaining a slope or marking a change in the direction of a path. Or they can simply add to the sense of an aesthetically balanced garden composition.

RETAINING WALL BUILT OF LARGE ROCKS AND BOULDERS

When boulders are used for a retaining wall, they should not abut each other, but rather overlap in an irregular, in-out pattern as if each rock were supporting its neighbor. Heavy boulders set deeply into the ground, with their center of gravity slightly tipped back into the retained embankment, create a secure and economic system of holding the soil above while permitting water to drain through its open joints. An open-jointed retaining wall of boulders is flexible enough to heave without impairing its strength in areas of severe winter frost. Over time it grows more aesthetically pleasing as its surfaces weather and lichens accumulate. Often such a wall is more economical to construct than a retaining wall built of reinforced concrete, blocks, or of rocks in an assortment of sizes laid up in closely fitted joints by a professional stonemason.

PEAKS

When the desired effect is a peak pointing skyward, set the rock at an angle of repose. In other words, it should look stable, balanced, not as if it is going to topple over. In nature, mountains do not appear to be trembling in the balance. If you set a dominant rock at an angle, creating a dynamic sense of movement, you should place other rocks leaning in the opposite direction to provide visual support.

When choosing a vertical rock, look at its seams. A tall, slim standing rock should "look vertical,"—that's to say, it should have vertical running seams rather than horizontal ones. Once the rock is in place, tamp the soil all around to insure that it is firmly anchored. In addition, for safety reasons, you should make sure that the center of gravity is tipped slightly backward, where the rock either can be buttressed by a supporting rock or by rising ground behind it. If the rock sits next to a shrub or tree, you may have to prune the plant so that it does not conceal the view of the rock.

STEPPING STONES

Set stepping stones so that the long axis of each stone is transverse, or perpendicular, to the axis of the path. Larger stepping stones, approximately two feet long, should be placed so that their centers are on the centerline of the path. Smaller stepping stones, however, should be staggered, generally following the axis of the path.

Stepping stones look best when they project about two inches above the finished grade. Thin stones may require a cement-slush setting bed to keep them stable. In order to convey a sense of stability and repose, set stepping stones so that their horizontal plane looks level.

A retaining wall of open-jointed rocks is both practical and beautiful. It is also flexible enough to heave without impairing its strength in areas of severe winter frost.

To slow the pace of visitors walking over stepping stones, create narrow joints, roughly four to five inches apart. Conversely, wide joints, six to 12 inches apart, induce a faster gait. Water the rocks as if they were plants. Dry rocks look dead.

POND EDGES

When setting rocks into a pond or around the water's edge, keep in mind the ultimate normal water level. Rocks should not look as if they have been drowned in a flood; neither should their "feet" (bases) be exposed above the normal water level.

Whether in water or in a dry karesansui composition, set rocks for an island in a pond so that their tops are not level with each other. In this setting, a large rock gives the impression of a rocky peak or mountain emerging from the sea; supporting rocks set around its base should be invisible, submerged as far as possible below the water's surface.

SEASHORE LANDSCAPES

For a seashore landscape, use rugged-looking rocks and place them in an irregular, disordered pattern, to evoke the turbulence of waves and high seas. Frame the view so that the first glimpse of the "sea" is through narrow openings between rocks, hills, or mountains.

Seeming to grow up from the garden soil, rocks represent to the Japanese stability and durability in a world that is transitory.

A waterfall looks more natural and interesting if the water tumbles down in a series of drops, each placed laterally off-center so that the water follows a zigzag course.

STREAMS

A rocky streambed must have a pitch of at least three to four percent if the stream is to have sufficient flow. To make the rock placement realistic, observe how, in nature, water flows more swiftly around the convex turn in a stream, cutting into the bank, while it slows down along the concave bend, where it deposits silt. To prevent erosion at the vulnerable convex points, set rocks jutting into the bank where the current moves most rapidly and forcefully.

Where rocks follow the banks of a stream or the shoreline of a pond, set additional rocks back away from the water in an naturalistic, irregular pattern, so that the rocks at the water's edge do not appear merely lined up in an unnaturally ordered series. Do not use many rocks along a slow, meandering stream flowing through a generally flat, level terrain. But do use only rocks that are flat and smooth, suggesting an old, worn-down, broad river valley.

WATERFALLS

When constructing a waterfall with a drop of three to four feet, use rocks that are rugged to give the feeling of mountainous terrain. Start

Placed along a streambank, rocks prevent erosion as the water careens around the twists and turns of its channel. To make rock placement realistic, observe how water flows in nature.

building from the bottom up. The fall will look more natural and interesting if the water tumbles down in a series of drops, each placed laterally off-center so that the water follows a zigzag course. Side rocks guide the water and, depending on how they are juxtaposed, can create the desired agitation and boiling effect. It will look more natural if the width of the "fall" rock at the lip of the drop is no wider than two feet. If the fall is too wide, it will look like a dam. Water should appear unexpectedly from a dark place partly shaded by plantings, as if it were emerging from a hidden source.

For a fall of many ribbons of water, make the rim at the top wide enough to enable you to place rocks in the stream bed to divide the current, causing the water to bounce off the stones as it gushes past, before dropping over the rim. Once the water has passed over low splash rocks at the bottom of the waterfall, it becomes calm. Consequently, the rocks around the water's edge should be smooth and flat, suggesting a quiet pool.

For inspiration, observe rocks in nature and study exemplary garden rock work. But beware of rules: slavishly following the injunctions and formulas found in design manuals will stultify your creative spirit, and you will end up with a stereotypical garden.

WATER IN THE JAPANESE GARDEN STYLE

JUDY GLATTSTEIN

WATER IS MAGICAL in any garden, whether as a still pool that mirrors the sky or a musical stream purling over rocks. This is eminently true in Japanese gardens, where water has spiritual and religious connotations. Shinto theology holds that kami, native gods, inhabit waterfalls and ponds (among other places or objects), and the calm, level plane of a pond's surface holds a special beauty. What's more, water, although absent, is suggested in the Zen-style karesansui, dry gardens of raked sand and stone. Ritual cleansing, important as a preliminary to the tea ceremony, requires that the highly refined design of a Japanese tea garden always must include a tsukubai, a hand-washing bowl. These gardens convey messages that non-Japanese may not be able to read. We see the beauty, but the language is not ours; the idiom is empty of meaning. Placing a tsukubai in a Western-style garden is form without substance, solely an ornament that does not make the garden Japanese. Likewise, a round or rectilinear Western-style geometrical pond plopped in the middle of a lawn and surrounded by a necklace of cut stone does not convey the reverence for nature of its Japanese counterpart. What is needed is a balance, the Japanese message in a Western vernacular.

The best (and most pleasant) form of garden research is visiting gardens. However, public gardens in the Japanese style tend to be grand affairs: the recently renovated Hill-and-Pond Garden of the Brooklyn Botanic Garden, Sansho-en at the Chicago Botanic Garden, Seiwa-en at the Missouri Botanical Garden in St. Louis, Fairmount Park's Shofuso in Philadelphia, and the Portland Japanese Garden in Oregon. In Japan, these would have been the gardens of wealthy nobility. They are beautiful places to visit, they inspire, and they overwhelm. Just as Japanese of more modest means have always had smaller gardens, Western home garden-

ers work with more inti-
mate spaces. And so when
visiting a public garden,
we must abstract a portion
of such a grand-scale landscape and apply its lessons
to our restricted space.

WATER GARDENS FOR CONFINED URBAN SETTINGS

Water in a garden, whether a tiny city garden or large rural setting, refreshes the spirit.

In urban areas a brownstone backyard, a townhouse courtyard/patio, or an apartment balcony may be the entire landscape. Water in such a cityscape refreshes the spirit, just as it does in a rural setting. A reflective pond leads the mind to reflection; the sound of moving water masks the urban uproar.

City gardens tend to be shaded, more often by surrounding buildings than by trees. Imagine a small spring in a shady woodland, a shallow pool of water emerging from the ground, its gravel bottom seen through the clear water, its edges fringed by moisture-loving ferns. Place your little spring so that it is partially concealed, for the enchantment of discovery is more pleasing than the blatantly obvious. The pool should appear to be lower than the surrounding area. (If it actually were lower, heavy rains would flush dirt and debris into it.) Use the scooped-out soil to create a gently graded slope away from the water, thereby disguising the grade of the area, which is probably flat. Natural stones arranged with ferns, a

Even the tiniest city backyard can become the setting for a stone water basin.

mossy stump, or a gnarled piece of driftwood can provide the necessary edging in an attractive manner. Remember to aim for the subtle rather than the flashy. Whatever stone you choose should match the sand and gravel on the bottom of the pool. Remember, too, that local stone provides a better "sense of place" than imported material (and is also more cost-effective). Choose moderate size, clump-forming rather than running ferns for your tiny garden. Evergreen Christmas fern, *Polystichum acrostichoides*, provides year-round interest, with silver-haired crosiers unfolding in spring that mature to dark green fronds. Deciduous maidenhair fern, *Adiantum pedatum*, has elegant, apple green fronds on graceful black stipes (stems). Mossy rocks and tree stumps need tender loving care, just as the ferns do, so be sure to match the amount of sun/shade in the garden setting to that in their original locations. Most mosses will remain in better health with periodic misting when natural rainfall is lacking.

A "garden apartment" is often the antithesis of garden, with a two-by-nothing concrete patio and perhaps a narrow planting bed wedged up against a fence. The space confined within the boundary of dwelling and fence is akin to that found in tsubo-niwa, courtyard gardens of the Edo period (1600 to 1868). In most cases, removing the concrete is not an option, so think instead of disguising it. In fact, disguise is the name of the game in such a garden. Cover the concrete with pine bark mulch; the dark surface will provide a more natural look, and keep the area cooler than heat-retentive concrete. Use stepping stones to form an S-shaped pathway following the long dimension of the area, or diagonally if it is square. If the fence is not attractive, consider hanging a bamboo blind to create a pleasant backdrop.

Interestingly enough, according to one interpretation, the character for tsubo means "pot," while niwa means "garden." Planting in containers is

For a more elaborate design, create a water drip using a recirculating pump.

thus very much in character for this type of garden, and compensates for the absence of open ground. It has the additional virtue of slowing the growth of woody plants by limiting their root run. Japan, more than any other country, relies on the use of native plants in gardens. We should emulate this approach. Striped-bark maple, *Acer pensylvanicum*, is a small tree with not only interesting striped bark but also tidy foliage and excellent autumn color. Mountain laurel, *Kalmia latifolia*, is a popular shrub with glossy evergreen leaves and attractive flowers in spring. Both these species are native to the forests of the northeastern United States. At the nursery, look for a tree with an interesting form, and a shrub that has not been clipped into poodle-ball uniformity.

Remember that in Japanese garden design, flowers are a seasonal addition used with restraint. One container to provide a shifting seasonal display is sufficient. And where, you ask, is the water? The restricted site, possibly viewed from inside more often than entered into, is the appropriate setting for a tsukubai. Set the stone basin in one curve of the path and place some taller stones to the side and lower stones to the front. If you want to elaborate the design, create a drip of water from a bamboo pipe, using a recirculating pump to keep the water flowing. Pair the plant containers, using them as a backdrop for the tsukubai, and set three large stones to "explain" the second curve in your path. Charming during the growing season, your tsubo-niwa garden will be even more appealing when dusted with winter's snow. If you garden in an area with mild winters, select regionally appropriate plants. After all, a Japanese gardener in chilly Hokkaido would use different plants than one living in subtropical Yakushima.

An apartment balcony is a difficult setting for a garden. Dwelling above the ground often creates a hunger for a garden, and yet such a site is limited in size, and weight must be restricted as well. In addition, water drip-ping from above can be a nuisance for the neighbors with the balcony below. In such a garden, water must be confined, and limited in quantity. A subtle movement of contained water spilling over a container's rim lends motion to an otherwise static scene. Attractive pots with subtle brown, burgundy, or soft green glazes imported from Asia are readily available. Their rounded outline and rolled rim lend a gentle, quiet appearance to the garden. Set the pot of your choice on a platform that conceals a water reservoir; a large plastic container hidden behind unpainted, rough-surfaced boards will do. Cross-braces and heavy-duty hardware cloth suspended over the opening support the pot and a dis-guising layer of cobbles. A pump submerged in the plastic container and the appropriate plumbing wired to a GFI circuit will gently send the water round and round. (Connect a plastic pipe to the pump and direct the pipe through the drain hole in the ceramic pot for several inches. Water spills over the rim of the ceramic pot, drips back into the plastic container, and is pumped up again.) Choose a small pump and adjust it not for a fountain but rather a soft roiling of water. Moving water also inhibits mosquitoes and their attendant problems. If you are tempted to add goldfish, keep in mind that they cannot survive winter outdoors in cold climates. And flush-ing them down the toilet or releasing them in public park ponds is neither humane nor ecologically wise.

A second container, filled with water plants, would add to the ambience. I've grown giant horsetail, *Equisetum telmateia*, in a brown and cream glazed pickle crock, which is appropriate in appearance. Set a plastic pot into the crock to hold the plant, and spread a layer of gravel over the soil to keep the water clean. Use scissors to trim the horsetail shoots to a uni-form level, which provides a cultivated look, a practice I once saw in a Kyoto Buddhist temple garden. Add a plain bench, a shelf for displaying a bonsai or a simple arrangement with a few flowers or a spray of seasonal foliage and you've created a minimalist scholar's garden where the harried city dweller can relax. Again, disguise concrete and walls, perhaps with a sisal rug to suggest tatami mats, and hang a bamboo blind as a backdrop.

WATER GARDENS FOR LARGER SETTINGS

Suburban and rural gardeners have more space to play with. They have more options, but also greater decisions to make. Designing a water fea-ture into a larger landscape can be complex. Water may be already pres-ent on the property, or it can be introduced. Let's first consider the luxu-ry of natural water.

In 1997, I attended the first intensive seminar on Japanese garden art sponsored by the Kyoto University School of Art and Design. A statement made by the school's vice-president, Amasaki-sensei, made a great impression on me. Gardening, he said, is about finding a balance between wildness and control, a distillation of the best parts of the natural world. Suppose, he went on, one took a piece of woodland, delineated the perimeter and then maintained it for a period of years, sweeping and so on. It would not be a garden in the conventional sense of the word, but it would develop the style of a garden. And this is just what I would like to address next.

In his early twenties, Chris Stout already has a gardener's eye. Along the bottom of his family's property in western New Jersey runs a tiny rill of water. The small creeklet, a couple of steps wide, is the sort of water feature that is easy to overlook. Barely flowing in summer, a couple of inches deep in winter, with a porous sandy, gravelly bottom, it is choked with leaves, twigs, and other natural debris. Basically, all Chris does is rake the watercourse using a folding metal rake with long adjustable wire tines. He does this approximately once a month in spring and summer, more frequently in autumn, when the creeklet needs raking about once a week until the leaves have fallen from the trees. He rakes gently, so as not to disturb the sand and gravel. Raking is also needed after a bad storm,

Using locally found rocks and native plants, you can transform a stream that's flowing through your site into a lovely garden setting. Finding the balance between wildness and control is key when attempting this type of landscaping endeavor.

In nature, ponds are often linked by a waterfall. For a water garden to appear natural, the site has to slope in such a way that the ponds appear uncontrived, intrinsic features of the landscape.

when lots of sticks and leaves must be removed. Chris told me he does not try to make the site immaculately clean. That, he feels, would look artificial. However, Chris did two things to enhance the little waterway: he built a low stone wall inside the creeklet to stabilize the bank. And, observing the rounded, moss-covered rocks lying within the channel, he added some additional stones that quickly became moss-covered, too. The effect is absolutely enchanting.

I have a larger stream which is a drainage creek, containing water only some of the time. Feeding into it is the overflow from a neighbor's artesian well, which does flow year-round. The stream has a mucky, muddy bottom. My plan is to emulate Chris Stout's little rill by widening the waterway somewhat, clearing the debris, and lining the bottom with gravel. However, more mud will continue to wash down and cover the gravel. Therefore, at the head of the area where I will be working I intend to create a sump, a small pit lined with two square concrete chimney blocks stacked one above the other. Mud and debris will fall into the sump, necessitating periodic cleaning. The sump will, however, protect the gravel from siltation.

Water gardening is now so popular in Western gardens that a couple of artificial ponds linked by a waterfall have become a common sight. Such

If the rock at the edge of a waterfall leans over its supporting
stone, creating a cavity between
falling water and rock surface,
sound will be pleasantly amplified.

gardens are often located in
an otherwise flat area, with
one pond abruptly elevated to
allow the water to flow into
the other, and a molehill of
earth arising from the ground
to simulate a mountain—con-
vincing naturalistic landscapes they are not, even if
you squint. These setups
remind me of nothing so
much as the water hazards on
pitch-and-putt miniature golf
courses: nothing about them
speaks of nature. Yet forming pond and pond, linked by a waterfall, is what
water does. For a water garden to appear natural, the site must slope in
such a way that the upper pond appears uncontrived, an intrinsic feature of
the landscape. Trees and shrubs can add verisimilitude by softening and
disguising the boundary. One difficulty is the typical Western perception
that bigger must be better—a large pond, a high waterfall, and lots of rushing water. A small upper pond, perhaps more of a spring arising between
some rocks, is adequate. And the waterfall need not be more than a foot or
so high, perhaps even less. If the rock at the edge of the fall leans over its
supporting stone, creating a cavity between falling water and rock surface,
sound will be pleasantly amplified.

Plants are important to disguise the edges of an artificial pond and create a natural transition to the surrounding landscape. Ferns are especially appropriate in a shady area, as is Jack-in-the-pulpit, *Arisaema triphyllum*, with its three-part leaves, unusual hooded flower, and sealing-wax
red berries in autumn. For part shade, consider umbrella plant, *Darmera
(Peltiphyllum) peltata*. Flowers appear early in spring before the leaves
appear. When they do emerge, the large pleated leaves can be over a foot

across. Sunny sites offer possibilities too: blue flag iris, *Iris versicolor*, has elegant, sword-like, bluish green leaves and smoky blue flowers in early summer. Sweet flag, *Acorus calamus*, also has sword-like leaves in a warm yellow-green, but has inconspicuous flowers.

WATER GARDENS FOR ARID CLIMES

Karesansui such as Ryoan-ji in Kyoto are gardens of stone and sand or gravel where water is present by implication only. Raked gravel provides the impression of waves/ripples in water around the "shores" of stone islands. This style can be appropriate in desert regions or other areas where rainfall is limited and water is precious. Envision a tiny streamside, a shallow basin edged with cobbles, with a small, low-flow pump sending the merest quiver of a ripple across the water's surface. Set this in a simple stone and gravel design. Enclose with an adobe wall. You are now ready to meditate on your Southwestern Zen garden from the veranda surrounding the courtyard.

One adaptation is to create a dry stream that not only looks attractive

Karesansui are gardens of sand and stone or gravel where water is present by implication only. Raked gravel provides the impression of waves or ripples in water around the "shores" of stone islands.

but also is functional, directing the water from occasional storms. An assemblage of rocks piled on the soil will neither look right nor serve any function in time of need. Excavate the dry stream channel and lower it below grade, to "explain" its place in the landscape. Look at natural streams before designing one: observe, for example, that a curve has a steeper bank where the water moves faster, and a lower bank where slower movement of water drops gravel and sand. The steeper the ground slopes, the deeper the water will cut and the straighter it will run. Plant roots are the best way to stabilize the soil at the edges of the stream. Suitable plants such as grasses and iris have linear leaves, which create a susurrus with each passing breeze and add to the pleasure of the garden.

Study Japanese gardens and observe how they create their sense of nature within a highly stylized design requiring intensive maintenance. Study nature in your area, and observe the interface of landscape, plants, and water. Combine the two, using indigenous material in harmony with the regional countryside to create a garden in the Japanese style with an American ambience.

The focal point of this adaptation of traditional designs is a dry rock "stream." Dry water gardens are especially appropriate in, though not limited to, areas where rainfall is scarce and water is precious.

PRUNING
TREES AND SHRUBS

DOUGLAS M. ROTH

GARDENS CREATED IN JAPAN are expected to last for centuries, and so the initial design and construction of a landscape are just the first steps in a long journey. The rest of the journey, 299 years out of the next three centuries, consists of guiding and improving the garden, modifying its design, fine-tuning it, grooming it, enhancing it. Although Japanese gardeners perform many varied tasks, the bulk of their annual workload consists of tree and shrub pruning. Thus, while Japanese gardening is a very broad topic, at its core lies the activity of tree pruning.

Why is pruning such an important task? Throughout a Japanese garden's life, many of its elements, such as rocks and gates, will remain fairly static. But the plants won't. Each year the trees and shrubs grow and change shape. They grow upward and outward, generally according to their own plant survival instincts. It is the gardener's task to guide this growth in the ideal direction. Far more than mere maintenance, the task of tree pruning is akin to carving out the three-dimensional shape of a garden. A tree's position in the landscape is determined when it is planted, but it is the skill of the person pruning it that determines what that tree ultimately will look like. If you consider how much of a garden's appearance is determined by the shape of its plants, you can see that the tree pruner is, to a certain extent, designing the Japanese garden as he or she shapes the plants year after year. For a Japanese garden to be successful, skillful pruning needs to take place every single year.

INSPIRED BY NATURE

One of the most important principles of Japanese garden pruning revolves around the respect and emulation of nature. Most successful

Right: Classic specimen trees are an important feature in Japanese gardens. They are usually thinned out in front to reveal the trunk and bark.

Japanese gardens appear to be natural and some even look as if they have never been touched by human hands. But in reality, Japanese gardens are some of the most tightly controlled landscapes on Earth. Other than the fact that they employ living plants, they are very far indeed from being "natural" landscapes.

Japanese gardens are inspired by nature but not natural. This is an important distinction. If a landscape is completely natural, it grows according to its own rules; strong trees prosper, weaker ones perish. Naturally growing trees develop according to the parameters of their environment, and factors like human scale or artistic beauty are of no consideration. Trees in a Japanese garden, however, are healthy and natural-looking, but they are encouraged to grow according to the gardener's instincts and not necessarily their own.

THE IMPORTANCE OF PRUNING

When pruning a tree—any tree—you should always prune for a reason. It's important to think carefully before and during the process. What is

The pruning of Japanese garden trees is such a detailed operation that gardeners need a stable platform for working. A tripod ladder with a telescopic third leg is ideal for pruning the top of a tree.

your purpose? What result do you wish to achieve? There are many good reasons for pruning, including safety, the health of the tree, and flower and fruit production. All of these considerations are important, of course, but in Japanese gardens, aesthetics play a larger than average role, and tree pruners must always balance the other goals with aesthetic concerns.

To understand the aesthetic role plants play in Japanese gardens, consider the topic of landscape painting. Imagine someone purchasing a fine landscape painting and displaying it in his or her home. Even if only for a moment at a time, the painting transports the viewer to that distant natural world, and he or she returns refreshed.

Japanese gardens play a similar role. But instead of being paint on canvas, the Japanese garden fills up a huge glass window along the side of a room or house. In other words, the garden is like a large, three-dimensional painting. Therefore, it is important to carefully consider the look of trees and shrubs, to make sure that their shape, size, and form satisfy the required aesthetic demands.

Many different effects can be achieved through pruning. It is possible to create moods of tranquility, delight, harmony, and natural ruggedness. For this reason, Japanese garden design has been compared to fine art. I respect this view, but I prefer to think of Japanese gardens more as a form of architecture—the combination of a building, a natural-looking garden, and people into the environment we call home.

HUMAN SCALE

The mention of architecture brings to mind the important concept of human scale. Consider how your house is built: doors and hallways have adequate width, stair treads are positioned with a certain offset, and your kitchen counter is set at a comfortable height. The average human body determines the dimensions, and well-built homes respect this scale. Likewise, well-executed Japanese gardens almost always respect the concept of human scale. Stepping stones are placed at standard intervals, ponds are located within easy view, and garden trees are maintained within a comfortable medium-size range. Consequently, specimen trees in Japanese gardens are often permitted to grow to a height of 12 to 15 feet, but usually not higher than that. It is the gardener's sense of human scale that determines how elements are positioned and how trees and shrubs are pruned.

The term "human scale" does not imply that Japanese garden trees are dwarf trees or trees that are kept at a miniature scale. That's a myth. Japanese gardens never involve miniaturization, and their elements are always full-sized. The landscapes almost always include mid-sized trees and even fairly large trees that float overhead. The height of a Japanese garden specimen tree is, indeed, controlled, but that doesn't mean the tree is tiny. In fact, most specimen trees are so tall that a ladder is required to prune them correctly.

SPACE CONSTRAINTS

Gardens built to a human scale aren't necessarily expansive. Japanese cities are crowded, and so Japanese gardens are often modest in size. A large residential garden in Japan would still be smaller than a quarter acre. Most gardens are much smaller, including some that are under 100 square feet. The gardener's goal is to make the most of these space limitations. Even if the garden can't be spacious, it can be special, a heavenly place on Earth.

Executing small gardens requires great skill. One concern, of course, is that putting a lot of plants into a small space is a formula for overcrowding later on. The Japanese solve this dilemma by using many plants and then carefully grooming each of them every year to ensure it fits its allotted space. In other words, the grooming given to garden trees is largely for shape and aesthetic effect, but much consideration is also given to controlling the size of a plant.

SHAPING SHRUBS

There are many different classic shapes in Japanese gardens, but two shapes in particular play important roles: the low rounded shape of massed shrubbery and the classic Japanese garden specimen tree. Many attractive gardens are composed only of those two basic shapes. While the classic specimen tree is very prominent, the element of massed shrubbery rarely gets noticed at all. This is ironic because low, rounded massed shrubbery plays an extremely important role in Japanese gardens.

In Western gardens massed shrubbery is usually used in foundation plantings, but in Japanese gardens it is found farther away from the house, where it can be seen from inside. Massed shrubbery is generally associated with azaleas, but any shearable shrub like boxwood or yew is also a good choice. Combined, such shrubs can form "waves" of foliage that give shape to the earth and offer enclosure similar to that of a hedge.

The shape of individual shrubs is semi-spherical, not round or ball-like. The distinction is important. While round, ball-like shrubs look false and out of place in Japanese gardens, shrubs pruned into semi-spherical shapes provide stability, mass, and tranquility. In this way, shrubs play a role similar to that of rock. Shrubs are often used in this way by garden-

Shrubs and trees are pruned to maintain size along the path in the Japanese Hill-and-Pond Garden at the Brooklyn Botanic Garden.

ers in areas such as Florida or the Midwest that are not blessed with an abundance of high-quality, handsome rock.

SHAPING SPECIMEN TREES

The term "classic specimen tree" refers to a particularly beautiful tree with a structural shape that is easy to see. Specimen trees are often positioned in front of a bamboo fence or white wall. They can also stand by themselves in highly visible spots, such as islands or at the very end of a

A garden that is mainly viewed through a window is like a large three-dimensional painting. Pruning should be performed with this vantage point in mind.

long, and straight path. Wherever a specimen tree is positioned, it is meant to capture your attention, and each tree has a strong influence on the garden's image.

Japanese garden specimen trees typically display a number of common characteristics: they have S-shaped trunks. They have cascading branches that emerge from the convex side of the curved trunk. They are usually thinned out in front to reveal the trunk and bark. There is open space between main branches. They almost always have well-defined "heads" that are rounded, not pointed, at the top.

TWO-NEEDLE PINES

Although other trees and shrubs are employed as accents, the main specimen tree in most Japanese gardens is the pine. Typically, pines comprise only about a third of an average garden's plant material, but how well these are pruned often makes or breaks a garden. In fact, this is the litmus test by which many true Japanese gardeners judge themselves.

Usually the main specimen trees are Japanese black pine (*Pinus thunbergii*). Many other two-needle pines can be used in place of black pine, however. Shore pine (*P. contorta*) and Scots pine (*P. sylvestris*) make good substitutes. Some three-needle pines would also work well. The main reason two- and three-needle pines are preferred as specimen trees is their growth habit. Two-needle pines generally have more irregular shapes, especially if they are out in the open and not in a forest.

This doesn't mean that grossly distorted trees are desired. On the contrary, in Japanese gardens, specimen trees should look rugged but natural. Avoid the temptation to select trees that look weird and distorted, or those that have been pruned into odd shapes. Avoid including any kind of false-looking topiary in your garden. Instead, strive for a Japanese garden that is tasteful, understated, and naturalistic.

TOOLS FOR PRUNING

Two tools are essential to pruning Japanese gardens. Hand snips are needed to make the many small detail cuts that are far too tight for Felcos or similar hand shears. The other essential Japanese garden tool is a tripod ladder.

The pruning of Japanese garden trees is such a detailed operation that gardeners need a stable platform from which to work. Four-legged stepladders are far too unstable and unsafe. Leaning an extension ladder against the foliage will break the branches. And climbing the tree is usually unacceptable because the tips of the outer branches are out of reach. It is possible to prune Japanese garden trees effectively using either cherry pickers or scaffolding, but in most cases those options are not feasible. For these reasons a tripod ladder with a telescopic third leg is an essential tool for pruning the top of a Japanese garden tree in order to limit its upward growth.

GETTING STARTED

There are a lot of English-language books on general horticultural pruning. These books point out basic pruning rules and encourage you to remove crossing branches, prune out deadwood, avoid leaving stubs, and so forth. Japanese gardening respects most of those common-sense rules, but goes well beyond them in terms of detail and aesthetic considerations.

When setting out to prune a tree, the first task is to decide from which side it will be viewed. In most cases, the main viewing point is the window of the main room in the house. Sometimes trees are viewed from multiple vantage points, but the view from the window is usually considered primary.

The side of the tree facing the viewing point is called the "front." As mentioned earlier, this part of a specimen tree is kept fairly open to allow viewers to observe the tree's interior and the character of the trunk.

Gardeners usually start pruning a tree at the top. During the pruning session, a large amount of debris will fall down, and pruning from the top enables you to clean off the debris as you work downward. Starting at the bottom is a mistake, because you will need to do a second round of cleaning to remove debris that has fallen on the lower limbs.

SHAPING THE HEAD

The top of the tree is called its head. Specimen trees usually have a well-defined head that is ample and rounded. The head consists of many branches that form an umbrella shape. There should be no central leader that dominates the head.

If a tree does have a central leader, remove it at the very beginning of the pruning session. This action may seem harsh, but it is a fundamental first step in creating an S-shaped trunk. If you allow the leader to dominate, the trunk of the tree will be tall and straight. By removing the leader Japanese gardeners create a rounded head. As the tree grows, part of the head divides into side branches, giving the gradually emerging trunk an "S" shape.

It is not necessary to use mechanical devices like wires, braces, or hanging rocks to twist a tree's trunk or branches into shape. This type of mechanical manipulation is common in bonsai, but it is not practiced in Japanese gardening. The trunk curves and cascading branches are created through "selective pruning," a general term that refers to the process of carefully removing woody material that isn't wanted

OTHER PRUNING TECHNIQUES

At least 50 techniques are used for pruning Japanese garden specimen trees. Most involve selective pruning. Two of the most basic pruning tasks are to remove all of the deadwood and debris from a tree at the beginning of a pruning session, and to remove any fallen needles and cuttings afterwards. Another important task is to remove all unwanted suckers and water sprouts, as well as branches that return toward the center (trunk area) of the tree. When branches cross each other or rub against each other, one of the branches should be removed. Branches that grow across the front of the tree, blocking the view of the trunk, should generally be removed as well. The same applies to minor branches that start to invade the all-important empty space between major branches.

Avoid creating "pom-poms" or "poodles," trees that have been sheared into topiary shapes, with round balls of foliage on the ends of stick-like branches. Although widely available in the nursery trade, they are inappropriate for a Japanese garden. If you have such a tree, try to flatten the balls and encourage growth outward and downward from the ball as well as along the bare branch.

One of the most important Japanese garden pruning techniques is to search for foliage that is growing outward and downward from the tips of main branches. If there is growth in this area of a branch, make sure not to prune it. Instead allow it to continue growing, and gradually the branch will cascade downward and outward. This cascading effect is important for three reasons: it makes a tree look graceful, natural, and old—highly desirable traits in a specimen tree.

It is extremely odd that one, and only one, Japanese garden pruning technique is well known to Westerners. This technique, called candling, involves snapping off fresh new buds each year in order to shorten branch internodes and restrict growth.

This technique is really only a minor grooming technique, and it can be counterproductive if applied blindly or too enthusiastically during the first decade or two of a tree's development. By removing or shortening a tree's candles you drastically restrict foliage growth, thereby eliminating many future improvement options. This is fine if a tree is already near perfect in both size and shape. But very few trees ever approach this ideal.

The pine tree on the left has grown according to its own rules. Through careful pruning from top to bottom every year, the tree on the right has been coaxed to develop into a classic specimen tree with an S-curved trunk, cascading branches, and a well-defined rounded head.

The shrub on the left has grown into an open natural form. The shrub on the right has been pruned annually so that its shape harmonizes with the surrounding rocks. Massed shrubbery is generally associated with azaleas, but any shearable shrub like boxwood or yew is also a good choice.

WORKING WITH NATURE

The most skillful tree pruners are patient and work together with the tree. They don't force their will upon a tree, but rather coax it toward the desired results. Japanese gardeners are sometimes thought to be highly manipulative, but this is a misconception. In fact, when pruning a tree, the best gardeners are often planning ten years down the road. The fact that they are willing to wait this long or longer for a desired result reflects great patience, not the desire to manipulate or force a tree.

Some Japanese gardeners say that the fundamental principle of pruning involves maintaining a tree's natural balance. They promote the idea of cutting back the strong areas of the tree while encouraging weaker areas. This is an oversimplification. It is better to think in terms of cutting back areas where growth is not wanted, and encouraging growth where it is desired. The difference is that a skilled pruner has a goal, and he or she encourages the tree to follow that vision rather than the other way around.

Still, the spirit of natural balance is valid in many ways. For example, a tree usually grows at the top. To maintain its natural balance, a pruner generally removes much foliage from the top and removes very little foliage from the lower limbs. This has a positive effect on a tree's overall health and appearance because the tree then invests more of its energy into the lower branches, which otherwise would slowly thin out and die.

Ironically, when the gardener returns to the same tree one year later, the foliage will once again be thick with new growth up top, and the lower branches will again be starting to struggle. Therefore, the process of thinning out the top and encouraging the lower branches must be repeated every year.

There is a perception in the West that pruning "hurts" a tree. To a certain extent, it is true—after all, pruning cuts the tree's flesh and amputates some of its living tissue. Pruning sets a tree back a little, and it takes time for the plant to regain momentum.

But if done properly, pruning produces positive and worthwhile results. Skillful pruning will, in fact, make a tree healthier. Sunshine will reach the lower and inside branches, encouraging healthy leaf growth. Pests avoid well-pruned trees because their openness promotes air circulation through the branches. Because Japanese garden trees are groomed every year, very little debris gets clogged up in crooks and tangled branches, so harmful insects don't find places to hide and fester.

When teaching about the care of woody plants in Japanese gardens, I always say, "Think about your teeth." At first this idea sounds odd. But think, for a moment, about the ongoing care a beautiful, natural-looking smile requires. It's not enough to be born with nice teeth. You need to brush and floss them every day. Sometimes you need to have your teeth cleaned. Sometimes you have cavities filled. A beautiful smile is a lifetime of work. So is a beautiful Japanese garden tree.

When contemplating Japanese gardens, Westerners too often focus on the lanterns and stone bridges and never look up to see what really makes a garden Japanese. Although it is vital to start with good design, proper engineering, and skillful stone placement, the truly critical element in a Japanese garden is human. More often than not, the success (or failure) of the landscape is determined by simple unassuming maintenance tasks like weeding and sweeping, together with the skillful annual pruning of garden trees and shrubs.

ENCYCLOPEDIA OF PLANTS FOR THE JAPANESE- INSPIRED GARDEN

PATRICIA JONAS

CHOOSING AND SETTING ROCK is the first step in making a Japanese garden, but plants are not afterthoughts. Plants have a formal design function and, as with rock, thoughtful selection and placement are vital. Good selection depends on knowing how each plant will fit into the design in every season and how it will help define the garden's structure and layers. Restraint rather than exuberance guides plant choices and the success of a garden often rests on editing. There is no room to poke in each season's hot new introduction or every division from neighbors' gardens. Herbaceous plants with their typically short seasons of interest and their habit of disappearing in winter are used sparingly. But evergreen and deciduous trees, shrubs, and groundcovers are vital, and even in gardens where the most austere plant palette is used, flowers may make a fleeting appearance.

Once the garden is in place, growth and change are subtle and controlled with scrupulous maintenance and meticulous pruning. Choosing plants that grow slowly, respond well to pruning, or attain a mature size in scale with the garden is wiser than fighting the plants' natural habits. In any garden, ignoring a plant's cultural requirements usually leads to weak growth and plants that are fatally susceptible to disease and insect attacks. In a Japanese garden, having to remove and replace ailing plants should be avoided: it results in scenes as awkward as mismatched plants in a formal knot garden.

Introduce plants not only for their individual beauty, structure, mass, and color but also for the counterpoint they provide to rock and

Japanese maples, ferns, and
azaleas, like those pictured
at right, are some of the
plants closely associated
with gardens in Japan.

for their evocative qualities. There are plants intimately associated with Japanese gardens—among them Japanese black pine (*Pinus thunbergii*), maple, Japanese apricot (*Prunus mume*), and the many species of bamboo and cherry—that have ancient cultural values and are rich with layers of meaning for the Japanese. Nevertheless, even without shared cultures, single plants can evoke universal scenes and create feeling by implying natural habitats.

In *Secret Teachings in the Art of Japanese Gardens,* David Slawson pointed out that natural habitat has been an important principle in Japanese gardening for centuries—at least since it was articulated in the 15th-century gardening instructional, *Illustrations for Designing Mountain, Water, and Hillside Field Landscapes.* However, it is not habitat or ecological gardening as we generally understand it; it is appropriateness to the scene evoked. As rocks shape or reshape topography and signify natural habitat, so are totem plants used to signify communities associated with habitat. Their role is to amplify the suggestion of habitat rather than faithfully re-create or restore it, as the following quote from the *Illustrations* as translated by Slawson in his book illustrates:

> In the planting of trees and herbs, you make their natural habitats your model. You will not go astray so long as you bear in mind the principle of planting trees from deep mountains in the deep mountains of the garden, trees from hills and fields in the hills and fields, herbs and trees from freshwater shores on the freshwater shores, and herbs from the seashore on the seashore.

Of course, even though you may take many liberties with the topography, remember that the landscape signified should fundamentally fit the site. Don't seek to change conditions that are unchangeable, such as attempting to evoke sunny hills and fields where there is only deep shade. Use plants only if they evoke the landscape scene you envision *and* are horticulturally suited to your site; cherries and bamboo are no more necessary to an "authentic" Japanese garden than are lanterns and bridges.

This encyclopedia is a mix of plants native to Japan and North America, but includes some plants common to other parts of East Asia and Europe. The temperate floras of Japan and North America have innumerable similarities and there are usually equivalent species within a genus that can be used to develop structure, mass, texture, and color—and that may be more culturally and personally meaningful.

Several important and beautiful native trees exceptionally well suited to Japanese-style gardens are omitted because they are so often fatally troubled by insects or disease—specifically, Eastern hemlock (*Tsuga canadensis*), tragically defoliated throughout most of its native range by wooly adelgid; American mountain ash (*Sorbus americana*), frequently beset by borers; and native dogwood (*Cornus florida*), which succumbs to anthracnose.

Not included are large canopy trees like *Cercidiphyllum japonicum* (Katsura tree), more suitable for very large gardens or parks. Also not included are many plants important in Japanese horticulture that have proven invasive in parts of North America: Japanese barberry (*Berberis thunbergii*), camphor tree (*Cinnamomum camphora*), spiraea (*Spiraea japonica*), and wisteria (*Wisteria floribunda, W. sinensis*), for example.

The organization of the encyclopedia is inspired by some of the classical habitats identified in Slawson's translation of the *Illustrations*, with plants divided according to four typical landscape habitats: Deep Mountains and Forests; Hills and Fields; Ponds and Streams; and Seashores. As Slawson points out, there are other landscapes (like deserts and prairies) that a 15th-century Japanese monk could not have imagined, but with ingenuity, this scheme can be adapted to any local flora. Finally, these categories also do not neatly coincide with North American plant provinces, so "Deep Mountains and Forests" might be Cascade Mountain forests or Adirondack Mountain forests, depending on the plant selection.

In addition to the plants described in detail, you will find more plant suggestions included at the end of each section. Some of these are discussed elsewhere in the book, in which case they will be accompanied by a page reference. Where appropriate, Japanese names have been included in addition to the botanical names.

DEEP MOUNTAINS
AND FORESTS

EVERGREEN TREES AND SHRUBS

Chamaecyparis
FALSE CYPRESS

Chamaecyparis obtusa (hinoki in Japanese) and *C. pisifera* (sawara) are very important garden plants in Japan, where they are native to mountainous regions. In the garden, they are used as canopy trees or pruned to low forms. They are moderate- to slow-growing and, depending on the variety, can have a mature height as low as a few feet. Hundreds of cultivars offer a range of excellent foliage texture and colors from dark green to bluish green to vibrant gold. They prefer moist, well-drained, neutral to slightly acid soil in a sunny but protected spot (Zones 4–8).

C. *lawsoniana* (Zones 5–7) and *C. nootkatensis* (Zones 4–7) are Western natives that generally grow taller in the wild than their Japanese counterparts. *C. nootka-tensis* can reach 100 feet in its native Alaska, but the extremely narrow form 'Green Arrow', for example, will achieve only 35 feet in the garden. *C. thyoides* 'Little Jamie' is a slow-growing dwarf selection of Atlantic white cedar native to coastal swamps.

Cryptomeria japonica
JAPANESE CEDAR

Japanese or Yakushima cedar (sugi) is frequently planted along the approaches to temples and shrines, where it rapidly reaches 60 feet and can grow to 200 feet and higher. It grows with *Rhododendron degronianum* sub-species *yakushimanum* on the remote, mountainous island, Yakushima, where it supports the timber industry. *C. japonica* is native to the mountains and

Chamaecyparis pisifera.

hills of China and Japan, where it has long been important both as a timber tree and in horticulture. It takes well to pruning, is tolerant of some shade, and is pest-resistant. Its reddish brown bark peels attractively and its foliage develops a bronze tint in winter (Zones 6–9).

Among its several hundred cultivars there are many dramatic leaf colors and textures and varieties with growth habits suitable for any size garden. *C. japonica* 'Araucarioides' grows to only 10 feet and is named for its resemblance to Norfolk Island pine (*Araucaria heterophylla*). *C. japonica* 'Sekkan-Sugi' slowly reaches 15 feet and has cream-tipped yellow foliage that turns

Cryptomeria japonica.

almost white in winter; 'Black Dragon' has dark green, almost black foliage. *C. japonica* 'Elegans', or plume cedar, grows quickly to 20 feet and has soft foliage that turns reddish purple in winter.

Kalmia latifolia
MOUNTAIN LAUREL
Mountain laurel (Zones 4–8) is native to North America's eastern deciduous and coastal plain forests of maple, hemlock and yew. It grows slowly to 7 to 15 feet in height, depending on the conditions and the variety. It sprawls more openly in shade, revealing the form and texture of its cinnamon-colored branches. It has a more rounded habit and flowers more freely in sun, but like rhododendron, it always needs its shallow roots to be cool. In any position, it requires moist, acid, well-drained soil. It will languish and be susceptible to the ravages of disease and attacks by insects if it is grown in inhospitable conditions.

Mahonia
GRAPEHOLLY
Mahonia is found at forest edges in North America and Japan, where it was introduced from China. The Pacific Northwest native, *M. aquifolium* (Zones 5–7) is not as tall as its Asian counterpart, *M. japonica* (hiraginanten; Zones 7–8), but both provide excellent multi-season inter-

Kalmia latifolia.

Mahonia aquifolium.

est and structure with their spiny holly-like evergreen foliage, fragrant yellow flowers, and dusky blue fruit. They prefer moist, acid, well-drained soil in lightly shaded, sheltered spots.

Rhododendron
RHODODENDRONS AND AZALEAS

There are over 800 species of rhododendron (tsutsuji), and extensive hybridizing has led to development of countless cultivars. There is a form and color for every taste, but most varieties require moist, well-drained, acid soils rich in organic matter. They grow in the wild in high and low mountains and on hillsides where their roots remain cool and never dry out. Among the species most often used in Japanese gardens are: *Rhododendron indicum* (satsuki; Zones 6–9), a semi-evergreen that grows in ravines and clinging to the sides of cliffs in the wild; *R. × obtusum* (Zones 6–9); *R. degronianum* subspecies *yakushimanum* (Zones 5–7), which grows slowly to form a tight 3-foot tall and wide evergreen mound; and *R. kaempferi* (Zones 6–9), which forms a loose, semi-evergreen, 10-foot-tall and 5-foot-wide shrub and is as vigorous as it is ubiquitous on sunny mountain slopes and hillsides in Japan.

Many species native to North America are also suitable. The fragrant pinxterbloom azalea (*R. periclymenoides,* Zones 4–8) is

Rhododendron calendulaceum, the flame azalea, has red fall foliage.

deciduous and native to Eastern oak-hickory forests, and the deciduous flame azalea (*R. calendulaceum*, Zones 5–7) has orange, red, or yellow flowers and red fall foliage that lights up mountain clearings in two seasons.

Sciadopitys verticillata
UMBRELLA PINE

This is a genus of just one species occurring naturally on steep mountain slopes in Japan, which is often planted in Japanese gardens (Zones 5–7). Called koya-maki, it can reach 150 feet in the wild, but is extremely slow-growing to 50 feet in cultivation. It has a beautiful multi-trunked form and needs little pruning, and seems to be untroubled by any pests or diseases. Its dark green needles are arranged in distinctive umbrella-like whorls, giving it an eccentric appearance. Although it grows naturally on sunny open slopes in moist fertile soils, at lower elevations it benefits from some afternoon shade. The umbrella pine is a distinctive specimen tree.

DECIDUOUS TREES AND SHRUBS

Acer
MAPLES

Acer palmatum or Japanese maple (momiji, Zones 5–8) is among the most characteristic of Japanese garden plants and is used almost as widely in North

American gardens. In Japan it is one of the indispensable plants of autumn, but the hand-like unfolding of its leaves is nearly as often described in literature as a signal of spring. It has an elegant broad-rounded habit that woody plant expert Michael Dirr suggests resembles our disease-prone native flowering dogwood *(Cornus florida)*.

The purple-leaved variety *(A. palmatum* var. *atropurpureum)* has perhaps undeservedly eclipsed the green-leafed form that has a lighter and subtler presence in the garden. *A. japonicum* (full-moon maple) is a common tree in the Japanese garden, but inexplicably it is harder to find in North America than *A. palmatum*. *A. japonicum* 'Aconitifolium' is the cultivar that's available most frequently; it is one of the most refined maples. Its spectacular foliage certainly rivals its *A. palmatum* cousins. Both *A. japonicum* and *A. palmatum* are associated with "Deep Mountains" and forest edges, so they may be planted in the distant "Mountains" of the garden. However, because they are also associated with "Villages," they can be planted nearer in, especially near a window where they can be admired.

Vine maple *(A. circinatum)* is a native with remarkable affinities to both *A. japonicum* and *A. palmatum*. With its cut leaves, the cultivar 'Monroe' is a ringer

The unusual bark of *Acer griseum.*

for *A. japonicum* 'Aconitifolium'. Although it is hardy to Zone 5 and puts on a long display of fall color, it is not often cultivated outside its native range. It is best in partial shade or the full sun of the Pacific Northwest, but it struggles to adapt to other regions' more intense sun in summer and winter.

Mountain maple *(A. spicatum)* is a small tree or shrub with beautiful yellow, orange, and red fall color; it is found in cool woodlands only at high elevations in North America (Zones 3–6). More adaptable to gardens is *A. pensylvanicum* (striped-bark maple or moosewood), native to deciduous forests of eastern North America and very closely

Prunus mume 'Tojibai'.

related to the Japanese species *A. capillipes* (snakebark maple) and *A. rufinerve* (redvein maple). Striped-bark maple is a small understory tree requiring shade and cool, moist, acid soil. Its common names are descriptive of its white- and green-striped candy-stick bark and, unfortunately, its irresistible appeal to moose and deer. Also useful for its exceptional bark and slow growth is *A. griseum* (paperbark maple), native to China.

Prunus mume
JAPANESE APRICOT

"One cannot enjoy the glories of the plum in bloom without having suffered winter's cold." There is some confusion about how to translate *Prunus mume*: it is usually rendered as Japanese plum (ume), but it is also translated as apricot, to which it is actually more closely related. With the flowering cherry and the peach, it is considered to be one of the three most beautiful flowering trees by the Japanese. Although native to China, ume had naturalized in antiquity, and so the German-born physician and plant collector von Siebold, who introduced it to Europe in the early 19th century, thought it was indigenous. The plum tree is a common theme in paintings, prints, and the decorative arts. As early as the eighth century, plum viewing parties celebrated the year's first blossoms with gatherings at which poems were composed.

This small tree possesses a rugged trunk that becomes gnarled with age and smooth bright green branches that emerge from the old wood, a poignant combination of young and old, particularly in the winter landscape. It is extremely long-lived (the Chinese claim specimens older than 1,000 years), making it a practical as well as richly evocative choice for the garden. There are hundreds of cultivars, with flowers in white and many shades of pink to dark red. The flowers have a spicy fragrance and appear in mid-winter before the leaves. Like the maple, ume is associated with "Villages" as much as "Deep Mountains," but in either case it grows best in well-drained, fertile soil and flowers most freely in full sun (Zones 6–9).

HERBACEOUS PLANTS

Actaea
BANEBERRY SPECIES

In late summer, as eastern North America's oak-hickory forests and beech-maple-hemlock woods hint at the blaze of autumn colors to come, native baneberries with white (*Actaea pachypoda* syn. *A. alba*) or red (*A. rubra*) berries grab attention closer to the ground. It isn't just their fruit that makes them choice accent plants: they have handsome foliage, grow slowly to form well-behaved, 2- to 4-foot-tall clumps, and are long-lived. They thrive in cool, moist, humus-rich soil in part to full shade (Zones 3–8). Although its smaller East Asian cousin (*A. asiatica*) is not commonly used in Japanese gardens, it is a striking companion to ferns and wild ginger, a more traditional herbaceous element.

Asarum
WILD GINGER SPECIES

Although the only European species of the genus, *Asarum europaeum*, dominates gardens, there are nearly 100 species of garden-worthy wild gingers, most of them occurring in Japan and North America. Throughout the long history of horticulture in Japan, they have been planted at

Actaea rubra.

shrines and temples and in residential gardens. They have also been cultivated as pot plants, where subtle variations of leaf pattern and their curious blossoms can be admired without poking around on the woodland floor. Cultivars of *A. takaoi* (hime kanaoi, Zones 6–9) selected for particularly rare and desirable markings are grown in decorative pots and sold for prices only Japanese gingermania can justify; a price tag of $1,000 or more for a single plant will not make a collector blink.

   A. shuttleworthii (Zones 4–9) is North America's showiest ginger and rivals *A. takaoi* for elegant foliage effect: it has handsome evergreen (or semi-evergreen) foliage with creamy white marbling and forms dense

Asarum canadense.

colonies in eastern deciduous woods from Virginia to Alabama, where it is native. Unlike the species, the cultivar 'Callaway' has smaller leaves, which are like those of *A. takaoi,* no more than 1½ to 2 inches long. The deciduous *A. canadense* (Zones 3–9) is more widely distributed across North America and has larger matte grey-green leaves that, although beautiful, lack distinctive markings. It is the hardiest ginger and spreads well even in inhospitable sites under shallow-rooted trees like maples.

Other gingers of note are *A. caudatum* (Zones 5–9), native to the Pacific Northwest, as well as *A. nipponicum* (kanaoi) and *A. blumei* (Zones 6–9), both native to Japan and possessing foliage so beautifully and individually marked that you might be tempted to consider pot culture. Most species do best in humus-rich acid soil with consistent moisture, although *A. canadense* tolerates lime. They grow in light to dense shade and are relatively maintenance-free. As a group, wild gingers are the choicest groundcover plants.

Mitchella
PARTRIDGEBERRY
This is a genus that neatly illustrates the affinities of the North American and Japanese floras. This genus has just two species: *Mitchella repens* (Zones 3–9), native to mixed deciduous and coniferous woodlands and clearings of eastern North America, and *M. undulata* (tsuru aridoshi, Zones 6–9), native to woodlands in Japan and Korea. With the possible exception that they colonize faster, what more to ask of groundcovers? They have glossy, evergreen leaves with a single, white stripe bisecting each round leaf and pleasantly scented, paired, ½-inch white, star-shaped flowers that give rise to single, edible (particularly to partridges) ruby fruit that persists through winter. *M. undulata's* leaves have a wavy margin, as suggested by the name. Both thrive in the wild in light to full shade with mountain laurels and rhododendrons and are also excellent companions for merry-bells and ferns.

ADDITIONAL PLANTS
FOR DEEP MOUNTAINS AND FORESTS

The plants in the list below are organized alphabetically. In cases where both North American native species (NAN) and East Asian native species (EAN) are suitable, the North American plant is mentioned first. Plants that are discussed elsewhere in this encyclopedia are accompanied by a page reference.

TREES AND SHRUBS

Amelanchier species Serviceberry **NAN, EAN**

Camellia species, p. 88 **EAN**

Cercis canadensis Eastern redbud **NAN**

Cercis chinensis Chinese redbud **EAN**

Chionanthus virginicus Fringe tree, p. 79 **NAN**

Chionanthus retusus Chinese fringe tree, p. 80 **EAN**

Clethra acuminata Mountain pepper-bush, p. 84 **NAN**

Clethra barbinervis Japanese pepper-bush, p. 85 **EAN**

Halesia monticola Mountain silverbell **NAN**

Hamamelis virginiana Witch hazel, p. 80 **NAN**

Hamamelis mollis, p. 80, *H. japonica* **EAN**

Ilex crenata Japanese holly, p. 84 **EAN**

Leucothoe fontanesiana Drooping leucothoe **NAN**

Leucothoe keiskei **EAN**

Lindera obtusiloba, p. 85 **EAN**

Ostrya virginiana American hophornbeam **NAN**

Ostrya japonica Japanese hornbeam **EAN**

Pinus ponderosa, p. 78, *P. strobus* Eastern white pine, p. 78 **NAN**

Pinus sylvestris Scots pine, p. 78, *P. bungeana* Lacebark pine, p. 78 **EAN**

Prunus species Flowering cherry **NAN**

Sassafras albidum Sassafras **NAN**

Stewartia ovata Mountain stewartia, p. 89 **NAN**

Stewartia monadelpha Tall stewartia, p. 89 **EAN**

Stewartia pseudocamellia Japanese stewartia, p. 89 **EAN**

Thuja occidentalis American arborvitae **NAN**

Viburnum prunifolium Black haw viburnum **EAN**

HERBACEOUS PLANTS

Disporum maculatum **NAN**

Disporum smilacinum **EAN**

Epimedium grandiflorum, *E. sempervirens* **EAN**

Shortia galacifolia **NAN**

Shortia uniflora **EAN**

Smilacina racemosa False spikenard, *S. trifolia* False solomon's seal **NAN**

Smilacina japonica, S. hondoensis **EAN**

Tiarella cordifolia, T. wherryi Foamflower **NAN**

Tiarella polyphylla **EAN**

Uvularia grandiflora Large merry-bells **NAN**

HILLS
AND FIELDS

EVERGREEN TREES AND SHRUBS

Pinus
PINE SPECIES

There are approximately 110 species distributed throughout the Northern Hemisphere, but the pines most favored in Japanese gardens are those pines with picturesque shapes that can be accentuated by pruning. There are pines at home in most habitats; even massive pines like

Pinus ponderosa, if well pruned, can be used effectively in "Hills and Fields" as well as "Deep Mountains." *Pinus thunbergii* (Japanese black pine, kuromatsu) is suitable to the hills and seaside of the garden, and *P. densiflora* (Japanese red pine, akamatsu) is suitable to hills and low mountains.

P. strobus (Eastern white pine), *P. sylvestris* (Scots pine), and *P. bungeana* (lacebark pine) are suitable for "Deep Mountains

Pinus thunbergii.

The bark of *Pinus bungeana.*

and Forests." Eastern white pine is one of our most beautiful native pines, but it will grow very fast to 50 feet unless kept pruned (and it takes well to pruning). Scots pine is widely distributed throughout Europe and Asia and has been cultivated in North America since the mid-18th century. It is extremely variable in needle size and color, heat and drought tolerance, and even habit. Lacebark pine is a slow-growing, three-needled pine from the mountains of China with beautiful mottled bark that becomes white over time. Groundcovers like *Mitchella repens* (partridgeberry, p. 76), ferns and club mosses that grow under a dense canopy of pines will help suggest that natural habitat in the garden.

Chionanthus virginicus.

The characterful *P. contorta* subspecies *contorta* (shore pine) and *P. rigida* (pitch pine) should be placed in the "Seashore" of the garden. Unlike more stately relatives native to higher elevations, shore pine is a short (to 30 feet), crooked, picturesque tree with dark bark, making it well suited to a Japanese garden. This tough two-needled pine, found on cliffs and dunes along the Pacific coast from California up to Washington, is hardy to Zone 6.

Pitch pine (Zones 4–7) is the signal tree of the Atlantic coast pine barrens and is even tougher and more adaptable than shore pine: it not only withstands the driest, sandiest, most windswept sites, but also flourishes in wet, acid soils. It has an irregular habit and dark, deeply furrowed bark when young that becomes smoother with age. Since *P. rigida* can grow to 60 feet, especially when not subjected to harsh coastal conditions, the cultivar 'Sherman Eddy', which grows slowly to 15 feet, is a better choice for a small garden.

DECIDUOUS TREES AND SHRUBS

Chionanthus
FRINGE TREE

Chionanthus virginicus (Zones 4–9) has all of the qualities one could ask for in a small specimen

Hamamelis mollis 'Pallida'.

crabapple has—except the insect and disease problems.

Hamamelis
WITCH HAZEL
Witch hazel is native to East Asia and North America, growing on wooded hillsides and at stream edges. *Hamamelis japonica* or Japanese witch hazel (mansaku, Zones 6–8) is rarely grown in North American gardens. *Hamamelis japonica* and the very fragrant *H. mollis* (Chinese witch hazel, Zones 6–8) are the parents of the beautiful hybrids *H. × intermedia* (Zones 5–8). From butter yellow to copper orange and brick red, their fragrant flowers are unmatched in winter; and their nearly horizontally extended branches provide beautiful structure as well. All of these shrubs prefer moist, acid, well-drained soil in full sun to partial shade.

H. virginiana (Zones 3–8) can be found throughout eastern North America as far south as Georgia and west through the central plains. Unlike its cousins, it blooms in fall, when its leaves seem to hide the source of the intensely sweet scent. It has a somewhat more irregular habit than the hybrids, making it less useful for defining structure.

tree: it has a graceful habit, elegant clusters of lightly fragrant, long-lasting white flowers, handsome and persistent blue-black fruits, and yellow fall color. One of its other common names, snowflower tree, describes the overall effect when it is in bloom. *C. retusus* (hitotsuba tago), or Chinese fringe tree, is a larger, less hardy tree (Zones 6–8) that easily rivals if not excels the North American native's floral display. In the wild, fringe trees grow in a variety of habitats: wooded hillsides, oak savannas, and streamsides. They tolerate wind but not drought. Although not traditionally used in Japanese gardens, the fringe tree has everything a flowering cherry or

HERBACEOUS PLANTS

Lespedeza
BUSHCLOVER
Bushclovers occur in Asia,

Australia, and North America. *Lespedeza bicolor* (ezo-yama hagi) is a shrub known in Japan as one of the seven herbs of autumn. The seven herbs or nanakusa are quite common in the wild and have represented autumn to the Japanese throughout a thousand years of poetry and painting. They also include *Dianthus superbus, Patrinia scabiosifolia, Eupatorium chinense* (formerly *E. japonicum*), *Platycodon grandiflorus* (p. 83) and two invasive species, *Miscanthus sinensis* (p. 94) and the pernicious kudzu (*Pueraria lobata*), whose starchy roots are used in cooking and baking.

Ezo-yama-hagi and its many varieties are widely used in gardens for their graceful arching form and beautiful pea-like flowers. While not the horticultural evil that *L. cuneata* (Chinese bushclover) is in North America, it nevertheless has naturalized in the southeastern United States. The very similiar Japanese sub-shrub, *L. thunbergii* (miyagino-hagi), or the completely herbaceous North American native, *L. capitata,* are good alternatives.

There are numerous splendid cultivars of *L. thunbergii* with lavender, rose pink, and white flowers. It is often slow to get started, but rewards patience in late summer through autumn with non-stop blooming. *L. capitata* has white flowers, is in bloom longer, and is generally

Lespedeza thunbergii.

shorter and more rounded than its Japanese cousin. It occurs in maritime habitats as well as in open oak woods on hillsides and in fields and prairies.

Lilium
LILY
Lilium auratum (Zones 5–8) is one of Japan's notable contributions to horticulture. It blooms with abandon during summer on sunny hillsides as its name, yamayuri or mountain lily, suggests. Its sturdy stems bear large, astonishingly fragrant white flowers with reddish spots and golden yellow markings. While the species is not commonly available commercially, it is a parent of today's Oriental

Lilium pardalinum.

Platycodon grandiflorus.

hybrid lilies like the popular 'Casa Blanca' (Zones 4–8), which shares its parent's intense fragrance but is pure white without markings. *L. speciosum* is another parent native to Japan and it too is an outstanding, fragrant garden lily.

These lilies thrive in well-drained, friable soil that warms up quickly in summer. Plant next to a rock with one of the grass-like members of the lily family that grow wild on hills and low mountain slopes in Japan: *Ophiopogon planiscapus* (oba-janohige, Zones 7–10) or the more hardy *Liriope muscari* (yaburan, Zones 6–10). Or plant it with a true grass like *Hakonechloa macra*

'Albovariegata' (Zones 5–9). *Hakonechloa* or urahagusa is named for Japan's mountainous Hakone region, where it flourishes like the native lily on open slopes. Any of these will provide some shade at the base of the lily, and permit its leaves and stems to be in full sun. Like many lilies, they are also suitable for pot culture.

The eastern North American native, *L. philadelphicum* (wood lily), also blooms in high summer and grows in open fields (Zones 2–6), where it may associate with bushclover. It also grows pondside and seaside, where completely different scenes are evoked. Other native lilies are the spectacular Turk's cap lily (*L.*

superbum, Zones 4–7) and the meadow lily (*L. canadense,* Zones 2–6), which begins blooming earlier in summer. The Turk's cap's natural habitat is wet meadows of the eastern United States, where it occurs with moisture-loving sedges and grasses; the meadow lily thrives pondside with ferns. The uncommon leopard lily (*L. pardalinum,* Zones 5–8)*,* native to California, is found in sunny sites in damp, humus-rich, sandy soil.

Platycodon grandiflorus
BALLOON FLOWER
Balloon flower or kikyo (Zones 4–9) is a genus of only one species that is native to grassy hillsides in China, Korea, and Japan. A much-loved flower for the summer and fall garden (it is another of the seven herbs of autumn), kikyo has been depicted in paintings and used in gardens for centuries. Like lilies, balloon flowers are often planted near rocks and also under trees, where they grow as happily in dappled shade as they do in sun. The flowers are lilac, white, and several shades of blue.

HILLS AND FIELDS

ADDITIONAL PLANTS
FOR HILLS AND FIELDS

The plants in the list below are organized alphabetically. In cases where both North American native species (NAN) and East Asian native species (EAN) are suitable, the North American plant is mentioned first. Plants that are discussed elsewhere in this encyclopedia are accompanied by a page reference.

TREES AND SHRUBS
Acer species Maple, p. 72 **NAN, EAN**
Amelanchier arborea Downy
  serviceberry **NAN**
Halesia tetraptera Carolina
  silverbell **NAN**
Juniperus virginiana 'Canaertii' Eastern
  red cedar, *J. communis* Common
  juniper, p. 90 **NAN**
Malus species Crabapple **EAN**
Vaccinium angustifolium Lowbush
  blueberry **NAN**
Viburnum dentatum Arrow wood **NAN**

HERBACEOUS PLANTS
Aster species Asters **NAN**
Epimedium grandiflorum,
  E. sempervirens **EAN**
Hosta species Hostas **EAN**
Mitchella repens Partridgeberry,
  p. 76 **NAN**
Mitchella undulata Partridgeberry
  p. 76 **EAN**
Patrinia villosa **EAN**

PONDS
AND STREAMS

EVERGREEN TREES AND SHRUBS

Ilex
HOLLY

Japanese holly, *Ilex crenata* (called inutsuge in Japanese) is a ubiquitous evergreen shrub (Zones 5–8) with hundreds of cultivars. Like boxwood it is used to lend mass to gardens in North America as well as in Japan. Native to Japan, it is often planted pondside and as an understory tree, but it grows natu-

Clethra alnifolia 'Rosea'.

rally in wet places in mountains and so is most appropriate for the "Deep Mountains" of the garden.

Equally good for planting in mass is the North American native, inkberry (*I. glabra*, Zones 4–9). Both of these slow-growing hollies bear black berries and are overall quite similar in appearance. *I. crenata* is less hardy and more prone to insect damage; but *I. glabra* has thinner leaves and tends to open as it ages rather than maintaining the very dense habit of *I. crenata*. Inkberry is found naturally in a variety of habitats: from the fertile soils of floodplain forests to sandy seashores, where it mingles with amelanchiers and bayberries.

DECIDUOUS TREES AND SHRUBS

Clethra
PEPPERBUSH

There are two outstanding natives of the eastern United States in this genus—*C. alnifolia* or sweet pepperbush, and *C. acuminata* or mountain pepperbush. Sweet pepperbush (Zones 4–9) is an easy shrub for sun or part shade with a rounded habit and panicles of cotton-candy scented flowers in high summer. It grows naturally near ponds and streams but will tolerate some drought and harsh seashore conditions. It slowly achieves a height of 6 to 12 feet, and its upright branching form is appealing in winter. Mountain pepperbush (Zones 5–8), as its name implies, is found growing on the tops of mountains and mountainsides in rocky soils. It also has a completely different habit, growing as a shrub or small tree to 15 to 20 feet with cinnamon-like exfoliating bark (thus its other common name, cinnamon clethra).

The Japanese pepperbush or tree clethra (*C. barbinervis*) is the most treelike in habit and elegant of the clethras (Zones [6]7–8). *C. barbinervis,* or ryobu, has slightly fragrant white flowers in 6-inch long panicles and a gray-green-brown patchwork bark that appears polished smooth. Its strikingly ornamental, exfoliating bark easily matches that of *Stewartia pseudocamellia,* to which it is often compared. Like *C. acuminata, C. barbinervis* is a specimen tree with year-round interest and should be planted in the mountains and hills of the garden, where it will get sufficient moisture.

Lindera
SPICEBUSH
Most species of spicebush are native to East Asia, but *L. benzoin* (Zones 4–9) is native to North America; it is a handsome shrub

Lindera obtusiloba.

underused in gardens. It grows to 6 to 12 feet with a rounded habit and occurs naturally in floodplain forests and along streambanks in the eastern United States. It is also tolerant of dry conditions. It is an asset to the garden in all seasons: in spring it is covered with fragrant star-shaped, greenish yellow flowers, followed by red berries, and its bright green aromatic leaves turn clear yellow in fall.

Two of the species found in Japan are *L. obtusiloba* (dankobai) and *L. umbellata* (kuromoji). Kuromoji (Zones 6–7) is comparable in size to the North American spicebush but is less hardy and its oblong leaves are longer. It has the same spring freshness, nearly black fruit, and even more uniform yellow color in fall. Dankobai (Zones 6–8) is called Japanese spicebush and is more commonly available. It grows naturally on mountains throughout central Japan and therefore should not be planted with the shrubs of "Ponds and Streams." It is considered a good shrub or small tree for the tea garden. Like sassafras, to which *Lindera* is closely related, its leaves vary from un-lobed to trilobed and it holds its fall color for a long period.

HERBACEOUS PLANTS

Farfugium japonicum
Farfugium japonicum or tsuwabuki (Zones 7–8) is one of

Farfugium japonicum.

two species in this genus that are native to Japan. Tsuwabuki is found naturally along streamsides and in wet places near the seashore. It bears fragrant yellow flowers in autumn, and its shiny green leaves are held up on long stalks, as if to catch random splashes of yellow. Where it is hardy, it is worth growing for its uniquely variegated foliage, which is particularly effective in shade. It is often planted in temple and tea gardens and is suited to container culture.

Polygonatum
SOLOMON'S SEAL
This is a genus of at least 50 species native to Eurasia and North America. *Polygonatum biflorum* (which now includes the formerly separate species *P. commutatum*) is one of four species native to North America (Zones 3–9) and is found in a variety of habitats: juniper hillsides, oak woods, and streamsides.

P. biflorum, P. × hybridum, and *P. odoratum* (the latter two are native to China, Japan, and Korea and hardy to Zone 4) are widely used in gardens for the elegance of their habit, charm of their flowers, and ability to form graceful sweeps in the garden. Arching, unbranched stems emerge from vigorous rhizomes in spring; soft green foliage that ages to straw yellow in fall unfurls along the stem; and small white, bell-shaped flowers tinged with green and followed by blue fruit dangle below the leaves (usually in delicate pairs in *P. biflorum*). Through most of their range, they will take partial sun as well as shade and mix well with *Actaea* (p. 75), *Asarum* (p. 75) and ferns (sidebar, p. 96).

Additional species native to Japan are *P. humile* and *P.*

lasianthum (Zones 5–8), which carpet moist meadows and open woods from sea level to low hillsides. Both are unusual in the genus for their small stature: the stems of *P. humile* reach only 4 inches and those of *P. lasianthum* reach only 8 inches, compared with the 3- to 5-foot stems of the other species mentioned here.

ADDITIONAL PLANTS FOR PONDS AND STREAMS

The plants in the list below are organized alphabetically. In cases where both North American native species (NAN) and East Asian native species (EAN) are suitable, the North American plant is mentioned first. Plants that are discussed elsewhere in this encyclopedia are accompanied by a page reference.

TREES AND SHRUBS

Amelanchier canadensis, Amelanchier arborea Serviceberry **NAN**

Carpinus caroliniana American hornbeam **NAN**

Chionanthus virginicus Fringe tree, p. 79 **NAN**

Chionanthus retusus Chinese fringe tree, p. 80 **EAN**

Halesia tetraptera Carolina silverbell **NAN**

Hamamelis Witch hazel, p. 80 **NAN, EAN**

Illicium floridanum Purple anise **NAN**

Osmanthus americanus **NAN**

Osmanthus fragrans **EAN**

Ostrya virginiana American hophornbeam **NAN**

Ostrya japonica **EAN**

Taxodium distichum Bald cypress **NAN**

Vaccinium corymbosum Highbush blueberry **NAN**

Viburnum dentatum Arrow wood **NAN**

HERBACEOUS PLANTS

Acorus calamus Sweet flag, p. 52 **NAN, EAN**

Acorus gramineus Grassy-leaved sweet flag **EAN**

Arisaema triphyllum Jack-in-the-pulpit **NAN**

Arisaema kiushianum, A. sikokianum, A. thunbergii, A. thunbergii subspecies *urashima* **EAN**

Asarum canadense Wild ginger, p. 76 **NAN**

Darmera peltata Umbrella plant **NAN**

Erythronium americanum Trout lily **NAN**

Iris versicolor Blue flag iris **NAN**

Iris ensata Japanese water iris **EAN**

Platycodon grandiflorus Balloon flower p. 83 **EAN**

Senna hebecarpa **NAN**

Sisyrinchium angustifolium **NAN**

Uvularia sessilifolia Strawbell **NAN**

PONDS AND STREAMS

SEASHORES

EVERGREEN TREES AND SHRUBS

Camellia
One of the most important economic plants in Japan and China is *Camellia sinensis,* which is rarely cultivated in Japanese gardens (although it is a handsome ornamental plant). *C. sinensis* is the tea camellia or cha-no-ki (Zones [6]7–9). Both green and black tea are made from its glossy, leathery leaves. The most treasured camellia in gardens

Camellia japonica.

and one of the most representative Japanese garden plants is *C. japonica* (Zones [6]7–9, but exceedingly variable). Even in the smallest gardens and Zen temples, where gardens are reduced to a few essential elements, there are camellias.

For many centuries, the Japanese have been breeding *C. japonica* (yabu tsubaki) and there are currently more than 20,000 registered cultivars. Camellias grow slowly to become trees, shrubs, and hedges. Where they are not winter-hardy, they can be grown as pot plants. They are prized for lustrous foliage, beautiful branching, and sumptuous waxy flowers that range from pure whites, pale pinks, and bicolors to the scarlet blossoms of the wild plants. Although now found everywhere in Japan, *C. japonica's* natural habitat is near seashores, where it grows in freely draining, evenly moist soil, protected from midday sun in winter and summer by the shade of pine trees.

C. sasanqua or sazanka (Zones 7–9) grows on sunny grassy mountain slopes and is more refined than *C. japonica.* It has less showy flowers, but when it blooms in fall, there is nothing around that gives its subtly scented, bright pastel or white flowers any competition. *C. japonica* flowers are often ruined by late frosts or an exceptionally cold winter even where the plant is hardy; but *C. sasanqua* puts on a long and dependable display in autumn (even into December) when days remain warm and temperatures drop at night.

Several decades ago, Dr. William Ackerman began crossing cold-hardy *C. oleifera* (Zones 6–8) with less hardy species at the United States National Arboretum. The result are tough hybrids with fitting names like 'Winter's Interlude', 'Winter's Joy', and 'Snow Flurry'. Shell pink 'Winter's Beauty' is a cross between *C. oleifera* and *C. japonica* and blooms from fall into winter.

Stewartia and Franklinia

Also in the tea family are stewartias (with species native to the mountains of Japan and eastern North America) and a small, elegant tree, *Franklinia alatamaha* (Zones 5–8), once found on the coastal plain in Georgia and now known only in cultivation. Both stewartia and franklinia have showy white flowers that bloom in summer over a long period and rival the camellia's. In fact, a Japanese native, *Stewartia pseudocamellia* (Zones 4–7), is called natsu tsubaki or summer camellia. Both have very hand-

Franklinia alatamaha.

some bark—franklinia's gray bark is marked by vertical fissures and stewartia's is irregularly patterned gray, brown, and orange as it exfoliates.

S. monadelpha (Zones 6–8) is also native to mountainous regions of Japan and is the tallest and least fussy of the genus. Like *S. pseudocamellia,* it has showy bark that adds interest in all seasons, beautiful white flowers, and deep reddish purple fall color. Mountain stewartia (*S. ovata*) also has camellia-like flowers and good fall color. It is found on streambanks and wooded hillsides in eastern North America in Zones 5–8 (at higher elevations in the southern part of its range), but unlike

SEASHORE

Viburnum dentatum.

its Japanese counterpart, it has plain bark.

Juniperus
JUNIPER SPECIES
There are 45 to 60 species and a bewildering number of cultivars of this conifer, but those most often cultivated in Japanese gardens are *Juniperus chinensis* (Zones 4–9) and *J. procumbens* (Zones 5–8), both found on windy hillsides and seashores in Japan. While they don't require pruning to attain desirable forms, they can take extensive shaping. *J. chinensis* is either a tree or shrub depending on the cultivar; and *J. procumbens* is a low, slowly spreading groundcover. *J. communis* (Zones 2–6) is the most widely distributed juniper found

in North America, Europe, and Asia, but grows naturally in alpine zones and is not as heat-tolerant as the Japanese species. It can be a spreading shrub to a small tree. Junipers require sunny, open sites and thrive in windy conditions.

Ilex opaca
AMERICAN HOLLY
The finest evergreen holly is *I. opaca*, an understory tree that grows very slowly to 40 to 50 feet, but more commonly to half that height. Old hollies can have contorted branches and a picturesque open habit that suits a Japanese garden well. *I. opaca* is native to the eastern United States (Zones 5–9), where it grows wild in maritime shrublands and mixed successional shrublands with serviceberry, pitch pine, beach plum, and lowbush blueberry. It does best where it is not exposed to drying winds, in moist, loose, well-drained soil. There are more than 1,000 cultivars, selected for dark foliage and the best berry production (berries vary in color from dark red to yellow).

DECIDUOUS TREES AND SHRUBS

Myrica pensylvanica
BAYBERRY
Native to the eastern United States, this handsome, all-seasons shrub is found naturally in

The leaves of *Arctostaphylos uva-ursi*, bearberry, turn blush red in fall.

the most challenging windswept seaside conditions, where its lustrous gray-green leaves harmonize with rock and sandy soil. It is deciduous to semi-evergreen in warmer parts of its range (Zones 3–7) and is useful for massing. Its leaves are aromatic, as is its waxy grayish white fruit that persists through winter into spring. Although it tends to sucker, it can be pruned to achieve a weather-gnarled appearance and to maintain its height and upright habit. Its natural partners are beach plum and pitch pine, and it also combines well with the groundcovering junipers.

Viburnum dentatum
ARROW WOOD
Often overlooked in favor of the showier fragrant viburnums, arrow wood is a very durable and adaptable native found in a variety of habitats from maritime shrublands to rich upland forests. It is useful massed and makes a good 6- to 8-foot hedge. It has lustrous dark green leaves that turn orange to red in fall; flat-topped, creamy white flowers; and attractive blue-black fruit. It does require management, as it will colonize.

HERBACEOUS PLANTS

Arctostaphylos uva-ursi
BEARBERRY, SANDBERRY
Bearberry is actually not a herbaceous plant, but a mat-forming, woody, intricately branching creeper that spreads slowly (Zones 3–7) in very sandy soils on exposed sites near

seashores and lakeshores. It tolerates salt and once established is drought-tolerant. It is a good ground-level companion to small trees and shrubs like gnarled pine, serviceberry, and high-bush and lowbush blueberry. When temperatures plummet, its dark evergreen leaves blush red, matching the perfectly round ¼-inch berries that ripen in fall. Small, urnlike white flowers bloom prolifically on the ends of branches in the spring.

There are several groundcover species native to California (*Arctostaphylos edmundsii, A. hookeri, A. nummularia*) and one to western Oregon and northern California (*A. nevadensis*). *Arctostaphylos alpina* var. *japonica* is the only species found in Japan; its habitat is dry alpine slopes.

Chrysopsis mariana
MARYLAND GOLDEN ASTER
Maryland asters (Zones 4–9) are very tough plants that grow slowly into well-formed, 3-foot-tall clumps covered in late summer with yellow asterlike flowers. They combine well with ornamental grasses and provide a useful display well into fall. They flourish in well-drained, sandy soils in full sun.

ADDITIONAL PLANTS FOR SEASHORES

The plants in the list below are organized alphabetically. In cases where both North American native species (NAN) and East Asian native species (EAN) are suitable, the North American plant is mentioned first. Plants that are discussed elsewhere in this encyclopedia are accompanied by a page reference.

TREES AND SHRUBS

Clethra alnifolia Sweet pepperbush, p. 84 **NAN**
Ilex glabra Inkberry, p. 84 **NAN**
Pinus rigida, p. 79 (Eastern) **NAN**
  Pinus contorta, p. 79 (Western) **NAN**
Pinus thunbergii, p. 78 **EAN**
Prunus maritima Beach plum **NAN**
Sassafras albidum **NAN**
Ternstroemia gymnanthera **EAN**
Vaccinium corymbosum Highbush blueberry, *V. angustifolium* Lowbush blueberry **NAN**

HERBACEOUS PLANTS

Farfugium japonicum, p. 86 **EAN**
Lespedeza capitata, p. 81,
  L. intermedia Bushclover **NAN**
Lilium philadelphicum Wood lily, p. 82 **NAN**
Viola pedata Bird's foot violet **NAN**

GRASSES, SEDGES, AND BAMBOOS

GRASSES AND SEDGES add texture, color, and a graceful, linear presence in the garden. They occur in virtually every habitat with the exception of the deepest forests, and naturally weave together other plants. Some are also among the most aggressive and difficult to eradicate if you find you've made a mistake.

Before you plant, check your Cooperative Extension Office for a list of locally troublesome plants. Avoid even allegedly well-behaved cultivars of federally designated noxious weeds, like *Imperata cylindrica* 'Red Baron'. Often used in Japanese gardens, heavenly bamboo (*Nandina domestica*) has escaped from cultivation in the lower South and is out-competing native vegetation. One of the representative autumn plants in Japan and a frequent subject of painting and poetry,

Panicum virgatum.

Muhlenbergia capillaris var. *filipes.*

Calamagrostis acutiflora 'Stricta'.

Miscanthus sinensis (suzuki) is showing up on state noxious weed lists, particularly in the eastern United States. To understand its invasive potential, one need only stand on sunny hillsides in coastal Japan, where *Miscanthus* can be the only apparent vegetation as far as the eye can see.

Although of smaller stature than *Miscanthus* and reliably hardy only to Zone 7, *Muhlenbergia* is an equally stunning focal point and a drought-tolerant native grass. There are many beautiful native species of *Andropogon, Calamagrostis, Juncus, Panicum,* and *Spartina,* one for every purpose. Sedges are among the best groundcovers for a Japanese garden; with inconspicuous flowers, short stature, and a plethora of species (more than 1,500), there is a *Carex* suitable for any site, small or large, wet or dry. *Carex dolichostachya* 'Kaga Nishiki' forms a neat 10-inch mound, has leaves delicately outlined in gold, and is native to woody slopes in Japan. *C. oshimensis* 'Evergold', native to dry woods and rocky hillsides and widely grown throughout Japan, has cream-colored leaves outlined in dark green and forms 16-inch tall mounds. But there are also many good sedges native to North America, like *C. plantaginea* and the widely distributed *C. pensylvanica.*

Many bamboos, even (and sometimes especially) the diminutive

Calamagrostis brachytrichia.

Bamboos must be contained.

ones, spread aggressively and can completely overrun the garden unless grown in containers or discouraged from running by 4-foot-deep impermeable physical barriers to prevent rhizomes from coming up where they're not wanted. Even then, keep an eye out for escapees and mow them down without delay: you can literally watch some bamboo species grow. There is nothing like the light that filters down within a 100-foot-tall bamboo grove and the papery rustling sounds even the gentlest breezes make. However, only large parks and palace grounds have room for stands that size.

Some bamboos are extremely invasive and should always be carefully contained, including *Pleioblastus auricomus, P. gramineus, P. pygmaeus* (Pygmy Bamboo)*, P. variegatus, Sasa palmata, Sasaella ramosa,* and *Pseudosasa japonica. Phyllostachys* is marginally less invasive, but still the ebony black culms of *P. nigra* (Black Bamboo) are best admired as a container specimen that can be brought indoors in winter (Zones 7–10). *Shibataea kumasaca* (often referred to as *S. kumasasa*) is a 3-foot tall erect bamboo native to Japan and cultivated for centuries for its beautiful evergreen foliage (Zones 6–10) and modest rate of spread. It is a good choice if you want to complete the pine-plum-bamboo "Three Friends of Winter" combination traditional in Japan.

GRASSES, SEDGES, AND BAMBOOS

FERNS
AND MOSSES

SAIHO-JI, OR THE MOSS TEMPLE, is one of the most famous and beautiful gardens in Japan. It was built in Kyoto in the early 14th century by Muso Soseki, a Zen priest who took gardening as his spiritual discipline. Its story is quite remarkable: it was laid out on the site of an earlier garden that was by then ruined; in 1467 it was leveled for the first time by fires, which were set repeatedly during a long period of civil strife; and finally, in the 19th century, it was allowed to go to ruin, so that slowly under ancient trees, scores of varieties of moss covered everything in a thick tapestry of soft greens.

The content and form of this ancient four-and-one-half-acre land-scape is the result of design, accident, and a unique cultural history. Although we have no comparable cultural landscape, we have natural landscapes to give us cues. Saiho-ji's dominant moss and the one most often planted in gardens in Japan, *Polytrichum commune*, also blankets rocks and trees in old forests and along streambanks throughout the United States. Except for the Pacific Northwest, there is no climate generally as favorable as Kyoto's to the growth of moss year round. However, there are about 1200 species of mosses in North America, flourishing in a remarkable range of climatic conditions. Mosses age and soften the contours of the garden, and at the same time they seem always fresh and new, especially after rain. Ferns are their perfect con-sorts (perhaps because both are ancient plants, mosses being the older of the regal pair); and under specimen trees, mosses seem to bring the faraway forest floor into the garden.

Moss gardens are not low-maintenance; they require as much care as any other part of the garden. A moss carpet may not need mowing like turf, but it is far more delicate, resenting air pollution and anything more than light foot traffic. Despite the illusion, it is a garden, not the forest floor, so leaf litter must be delicately swept away or it will smoth-er sections of the carpet; and it must be carefully weeded or it will be overtaken. Even with daily care, it will be necessary to reweave sec-tions of the carpet as conditions change and one species or another ceases to flourish or squirrels or deer tear up sections.

The easiest way to establish a moss carpet is to purchase or collect

Mosses age and soften the contours of the garden and look fresh at the same time.

(legally and preferably after a rain) moss plugs or sod, and plant immediately on a very acid, well-prepared, wet soil in conditions similar to which the moss has grown. Many mosses also take well to drying, crumbling, and sprinkling over areas to be covered. Both methods require that the moss be kept constantly moist until it takes hold—after which most species can tolerate occasional drying out.

For a number of handy formulas to get moss growing as a patina and in a variety of other situations, see "Moss Mavens" by J. Skuba in *The Journal of Japanese Gardening*, May/June 1999. For most gardeners, the subject is well and completely covered in *Moss Gardening* by George Schenk (see "For More Information," page 104).

A few recommended species, all of which may be purchased commercially (see "Suppliers," page 100), are briefly described below:

Dicranum flagellare, D. scoparium
This is a moss that conveniently stays green regardless of drought. It ranges across North America, growing in dappled light to deep shade, in average to moist conditions, on soil, rock, ledges, and tree stumps.

Hypnum imponens
Another easy-to-transplant moss, which Schenk describes as "talon-

FERNS AND MOSSES

Osmunda cinnamomea.

Lycopodium.

leaved." It thrives in dappled light to complete shade, on soil, rocks, and rotting logs.

Leucobryum glaucum
Found throughout the world in open woods and on the margins of swamps, these subtly colored pale blue-green to almost white cushions grow in shade to partial shade on dry to moist soils.

Polytrichum commune, P. juniperinum, P. piliferum
These three are found throughout much of the world, adapt to a wide variety of soils, thrive in sun or shade, and are easily transplanted. In the most favorable conditions (wet, rich soils), *P. commune* may stretch to over a foot, *P. juniperinum* to half that, and *P. piliferum* to several inches.

FERNS
Fern consorts are best chosen from among those that grow regionally, but here are some of the best, all commercially available and with the greatest distributions and hardiness zones:

Athyrium filix-femina Lady fern, *A. niponicum* Japanese painted fern
Dryopteris species Buckler fern
Matteuccia struthiopteris Ostrich fern
Osmunda cinnamomea Cinnamon fern, *O. japonica, O. regalis* Royal fern
Thelypteris novaeboracensis New York fern

USDA HARDINESS ZONE MAP

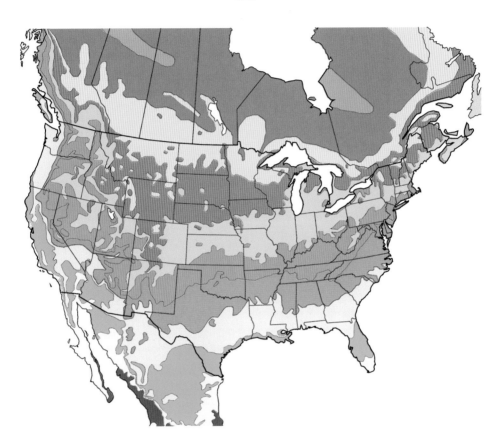

ZONES & TEMPERATURES (°F)

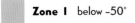 **Zone 1** below –50°   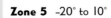 **Zone 5** –20° to 10°   **Zone 9** 20° to 30°

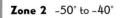 **Zone 2** –50° to –40°   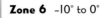 **Zone 6** –10° to 0°   **Zone 10** 30° to 40°

Zone 3 –40° to –30°   **Zone 7** 0° to 10°   **Zone 11** above 40°

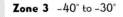 **Zone 4** –30° to –20°   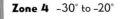 **Zone 8** 10° to 20°

SUPPLIERS

TREES, SHRUBS AND HERBACEOUS PLANTS

ARBORVILLAGE
P.O. Box 227
Holt, MO 64048
816-264-3911
816-264-3760 fax
arborvillage@aol.com

ASIATICA
P.O. Box 270
Lewisberry, PA 17339
717-938-8677
717-938-0771 fax
asiatica@ezonline.com
www.asiatica-pa.com

BLUE MEADOW FARM
184 Meadow Road
Montague, MA 01351
413-367-2394
413-367-0116 fax

CAMELLIA FOREST NURSERY
9701 Carrie Road
Chapel Hill, NC 27516
919-968-0504
919-960-7690 fax
camforest@aol.com
www.camforest.com

COLLECTOR'S NURSERY
16804 NE 102nd Avenue
Battle Ground, WA 98604
360-574-3832
360-571-8540 fax
dianar@collectorsnursery.com
www.collectorsnursery.com

DIGGING DOG NURSERY
P.O. Box 471
Albion, CA 95410
707-937-1130
707-937-2480 fax
dwhigham@diggingdog.com
www.diggingdog.com

EASTERN PLANT SPECIALTIES
P.O. Box 226
Georgetown, ME 04548
732-382-2508
732-382-2508 fax
www.easternplant.com

ECO-GARDENS
P.O. Box 1227
Decatur, GA 30031
404-294-6468
404-294-8173 fax
eco-gardens@mindspring.com

ENSATA GARDENS
9823 E. Michigan Ave.
Galesburg, MI 49053
616-665-7500
616-665-7500 fax
ensata@aol.com
www.ensata.com

FAIRWEATHER GARDENS
P.O. Box 330
Greenwich, NJ 08323
856-451-6261
856-451-0303 fax
www.fairweathergardens.com

FANTASTIC PLANTS
5865 Steeplechase Drive
Bartlett, TN 38134-5509
800-967-1912
901-372-6818 fax
fanplant@aol.com
www.fantasticplants.com

FORESTFARM
990 Tetherow Road
Williams, OR 97544-9599
541-846-7269
541-846-6963 fax
forestfarm@rvi.net
www.forestfarm.com

GARDENS NORTH
5984 Third Line Road North
North Gower, Ont. K0A 2T0, Canada
613-489-0065
613-489-1208 fax
info@gardensnorth.com
www.gardensnorth.com

GREER GARDENS
1280 Goodpasture Island Road
Eugene, OR 97401-1794
541-686-8266
541-686-0910 fax
orders@greergardens.com
www.greergardens.com

HERONSWOOD NURSERY
7530 NE 288th Street
Kingston, WA 98346-9502
360-297-4172
360-297-8321 fax
heronswood@silverlink.net
www.heronswood.com

LAS PILITAS NURSERY
3232 Las Pilitas Road
Santa Margarita, CA 93453
805-438-5992
805-438-5993 fax
bawilson@laspilitas.com

MATSU-MOMIJI NURSERY
Route 2, Box 147-D
Hurricane, WV 25526
304-562-9666
www.matsumomiji.com

MINIATURE PLANT KINGDOM
4125 Harrison Grade Road
Sebastopol, CA 95472
707-874-2233
707-874-3242 fax
mpk@neteze.com
www.miniplantkingdom.com

MOUNTAIN MAPLES
P.O. Box 1329
Laytonville, CA 95454-1329
888-707-6522
707-984-7433 fax
mtmaples@mcn.org
www.mountainmaples.com

NICHE GARDENS
1111 Dawson Road
Chapel Hill, NC 27516
919-967-0078
919-967-4026 fax
mail@nichegdn.com
www.nichegdn.com

PLANT DELIGHTS NURSERY, INC.
9241 Sauls Road
Raleigh, NC 27603
919-772-4794
919-662-0370 fax
office@plantdelights.com
www.plantdelights.com

PRAIRIE MOON NURSERY
Route 3, Box 163
Winona, MN 55987
507-452-1362
507-454-5238 fax
pmnrsy@luminet.net
www.prairiemoonnursery.com

PRAIRIE NURSERY
P.O. Box 306
Westfield, WI 53964-0306
800-476-9453
608-296-2741 fax
cs@prairienursery.com
www.prairienursery.com

ROSLYN NURSERY
211 Burrs Lane
Dix Hills, NY 11746
631-643-9347
631-427-0894 fax
roslyn@roslynnursery.com
www.roslynnursery.com

SISKIYOU RARE PLANT NURSERY
2825 Cummings Road
Medford, OR 97501
541-772-6846
541-772-4917 fax
srpn@wave.net
www.wave.net/upg/srpn

TRIPPLE BROOK FARM
37 Middle Road
Southampton, MA 01073
413-527-4626
413-527-9853 fax
info@tripplebrookfarm.com
www.tripplebrookfarm.com

WE-DU NURSERIES
2055 Polly Spout Road
Marion, NC 28752-7349
828-738-8300
828-738-8131 fax
wedu@wnclink.com
www.we-du.com

WHITNEY GARDENS & NURSERY
P.O. Box 170
Brinnon, WA 98320-0080
800-952-2404
360-796-4411
360-796-3556 fax
info@whitneygardens.com
www.whitneygardens.com

WINTERGARDEN AT GREEN NURSERIES
415 North Greeno Road
Fairhope, AL 36532
334-928-8469 (also fax)

WOODLANDERS, INC.
1128 Colleton Avenue
Aiken, SC 29801
803-648-7522 (also fax)
woodland@triplet.net
www.woodlanders.net

YUCCA DO NURSERY, INC.
P.O. Box 907
Hempstead, TX 77445
979-826-4580
yuccado@nettexas.net
www.yuccado.com

In addition to the following specialty nurseries, many of the above nurseries are also sources for bulbs, ferns, and mosses, as well as bamboo and ornamental grasses.

BULBS

BRENT AND BECKY'S BULBS
7463 Heath Trail
Gloucester, VA 23061
877-661-2852
804-693-9436 fax
www.brentandbeckysbulbs.com

THE LILY GARDEN
4902 NE 147th Ave.
Vancouver, WA 98682
360-253-6273
360-253-2512 fax
Thelilygdn@aol.com
www.thelilygarden.com

McCLURE & ZIMMERMAN
108 W. Winnebago Street
P.O. Box 368
Friesland, WI 53935-0368
800-883-6998
800-374-6120 fax
info@mzbulb.com
www.mzbulb.com

OLD HOUSE GARDENS-HEIRLOOM BULBS
536 Third Street
Ann Arbor, MI 48103-4957
734-995-1486
734-995-1687 fax
ohgbulbs@aol.com
www.oldhousegardens.com

FERNS AND MOSSES

FANCY FRONDS
P.O. Box 1090
Gold Bar, WA 98251-1090
360-793-1472
360-793-4243 fax
Judith@fancyfronds.com
www.fancyfronds.com

STICKS AND STONES FARM
197 Huntingtown Road
Newtown, CT 06470
moss@sticksandstonesfarm.com
www.sticksandstonesfarm.com

BAMBOO AND ORNAMENTAL GRASSES

BAMBOO SOURCERY
666 Wagnon Road
Sebastopol, CA 95472
707-823-5866
707-829-8106 fax
source@bamboo.nu
www.bamboo.nu

BLUEMEL, KURT, INC.
2740 Greene Lane
Baldwin, MD 21013-9523
800-498-1560
410-557-9785 fax
bluemels@aol.com
www.bluemel.com

ENDANGERED SPECIES
23280 Stephanie
Perris, CA 92570
909-943-0990
909-943-9199 fax
nursery@endangeredspecies.com
www.endangeredspecies.com

GIB AND DIANE COOPER
TRADEWINDS BAMBOO NURSERY
28446 Hunter Creek Loop
Gold Beach, OR 97444
541-247-0835 (also fax)
gib@bamboodirect.com
www.bamboodirect.com

NEW ENGLAND BAMBOO COMPANY
5 Granite Street
Rockport, MA 01966
978-546-3581
derosa@shore.net
www.newengbamboo.com

TOOLS AND ACCESSORIES

CHERRY BLOSSOM GARDENS.COM
Route 1, Box 301-B
New Prague, MN 56071
877-226-4387
952-758-1922 fax
www.cherryblossomgardens.com

PEACEFUL VALLEY FARM SUPPLY
P.O. Box 2209
Grass Valley, CA 95945
888-784-1722
530-272-4794 fax
contact@groworganic.com
www.groworganic.com

STONE FOREST
P.O. Box 2840
Santa Fe, NM 87504
505-986-8883
505-982-2712 fax
sfi@stoneforest.com
www.stoneforest.com

STONE LANTERN DISCOVERIES
P.O. Box 816
Sudbury, MA 01776
800-776-1167
978-443-9115 fax
inform@stonelantern.com
www.stonelantern.com

FOR MORE INFORMATION

JAPANESE GARDENS: DESIGN AND MEANING
Mitchell Bring & Josse Wayembergh
McGraw Hill, New York, 1981

LANDSCAPE GARDENING IN JAPAN
Josiah Conder
Kelly & Walsh, Tokyo, 1893

JAPONICA MAGNIFICA
Don Elick and Raymond Booth
Sagapress/Timber Press, Portland
OR, 1992

A THOUSAND MOUNTAINS, A MILLION HILLS: CREATING THE ROCK WORK OF JAPANESE GARDENS
David Engel
Japan Publications, Tokyo, 1995

JAPANESE GARDENS FOR TODAY
David Engel
Charles E. Tuttle, Rutland, VT, 1959

JAPANESE RESIDENCES AND GARDENS: A TRADITION OF INTEGRATION
Michio Fujioka
Kodansha International, Tokyo and
New York, 1982

ENHANCE YOUR GARDEN WITH JAPANESE PLANTS
Judy Glattstein
Kodansha International, New York
and Tokyo, 1996

THE EXPLORER'S GARDEN
Daniel J. Hinkley
Timber Press, Portland, OR, 1999

THE OCEAN IN THE SAND
Mark Holburn
Shambhala, Boulder, 1978

THE GARDENS OF JAPAN
Teiji Itoh
Kodansha International, Tokyo and
New York, 1984

SPACE AND ILLUSION IN THE JAPANESE GARDEN
Teiji Itoh
Weatherhill, New York, 1973

JAPANESE GARDEN DESIGN
Marc Peter Keane
Charles E. Tuttle, Rutland, VT, 1996

GARDEN PLANTS IN JAPAN
Fumio Kitamura & Yurio Ishizu
Kokusai Bunka Shinkokai, Tokyo
1963

THE WORLD OF THE JAPANESE GARDEN
Loraine Kuck
Weatherhill, New York and Tokyo
1968 and 1980

JAPANESE STYLE GARDENS OF THE PACIFIC WEST COAST
Melba Levick & Kendall Brown
Rizzoli, New York, 1999

THE INWARD GARDEN
Julie Moir Messervy
Little Brown, Boston 1995

THE JAPANESE COURTYARD GARDEN
Katsuhiko Mizuno
Tsuboniwa, Kyoto Shoin, 1991

INFINITE SPACES: THE ART & WISDOM OF THE JAPANESE GARDEN
Edited by Joe Earle
Charles E. Tuttle, Rutland, VT, 2000

**KATSURA:
A PRINCELY RETREAT**
Takeshi Nishikawa & Akira Naito
Kodansha International, Tokyo and
New York, 1977

FLORA OF JAPAN
Jisaburo Ohwi
Smithsonian Institution, Washington
D.C., 1984

REFLECTIONS OF THE SPIRIT: JAPANESE GARDENS IN AMERICA
Maggie Oster
Dutton, New York, 1993

AMERICAN PLANTS FOR AMERICAN GARDENS
Edith A. Roberts & Elsa Rehmann
University of Georgia Press, Athens
reissue, 1996

CREATING YOUR OWN JAPANESE GARDEN
Takashi Sawano
Kodansha International, New York
and Tokyo, 1996

MOSS GARDENING
George Schenk
Timber Press, Portland, OR, 1997

THE COMPLETE SHADE GARDENER
George Schenk
Houghton Mifflin, Boston, 1991

A JAPANESE TOUCH FOR YOUR GARDEN
Kiyoshi Seike & Masanobu Kudo with
David H. Engel
Kodansha International, Tokyo and
New York, 1980

SECRET TEACHINGS IN THE ART OF JAPANESE GARDENS
David Slawson
Kodansha International, Tokyo and
New York, 1987

THE GARDEN PLANTS OF CHINA
Peter Valder
Timber Press, Portland, OR, 1999

**JAPANESE MAPLES:
MOMIJI AND KAEDE**
J. D. Vertrees & Hideo Suzuki
Timber Press, Portland, OR, 1989

JAPANESE GARDENING IN SMALL SPACES
Isao Yoshikawa
Japan Publications, Tokyo, 1997

THE GARDENER'S GUIDE TO GROWING TEMPERATE BAMBOOS
Michael Bell
Timber Press, Portland, OR, 2000

NATIVE TREES SHRUBS AND VINES FOR URBAN & RURAL AMERICA
Gary L. Hightshoe
John Wiley & Sons, New York, 1988

NORTH AMERICAN LANDSCAPE TREES
Arthur Lee Jacobson
Ten Speed Press, Berkeley, 1996

CONIFERS OF CALIFORNIA
Ronald M. Lanner
Cachuma Press, Los Olivos, CA, 1999

IN THE JAPANESE GARDEN
Michael Yamashita & Elizabeth Bibb
Starwood Publishing, Washington,
D.C., 1991

MAGIC OF TREES AND STONES
Katsuo Saito & Sadaji Wada
Japan Publications. Tokyo, 1964

ROTH TEI-EN'S JOURNAL OF JAPANESE GARDENING
P.O. Box 159
Orefield, PA 18069
www.rothteien.com

JGARDEN: THE JAPANESE GARDEN DATABASE
www.jgarden.org

CONTRIBUTORS

DAVID HARRIS ENGEL, an American landscape architect and partner emeritus of the New York firm Landgarden, now resides in Chiangmai, Thailand. After graduating from the University of Michigan and Columbia University, Mr. Engel, under the auspices of Tokyo University of Fine Arts, worked with Tansai Sano, the master landscape architect of Kyoto. A Fellow of the American Society of Landscape Architects, David Engel lectures widely and is the author of *Japanese Gardens for Today, Creating a Chinese Garden, A Thousand Mountains, A Million Hills—Creating the Rockwork of Japanese Gardens,* and *What's That Tree—A Field Guide to Tropical Plants of Asia* and co-author of *A Japanese Touch for Your Garden.*

JUDY GLATTSTEIN is a garden consultant, author, and lecturer. *Waterscaping: Plants and Ideas for Natural and Created Water Gardens* (Storey Communications, 1994) and *Enhance Your Garden with Japanese Plants* (Kodansha America, 1997) are two of her six garden books. She has lectured across the United States and abroad, including Kyoto, Japan, and the Royal Horticultural Society's Great Autumn Show in London. She is a regular contributor to the Brooklyn Botanic Garden handbooks.

PATRICIA JONAS is a horticulturist, writer, and director of library services at Brooklyn Botanic Garden. She studied and visited Japanese gardens while living in Japan for two years.

MARC PETER KEANE is a graduate of Cornell University's Department of Landscape Architecture. He has made Kyoto his home for the past 15 years, first as a research fellow of Kyoto University, now as a landscape architect and writer. His design work includes private residences, company grounds, and temple gardens. Keane is also a lecturer in the Department of Environmental Design at the Kyoto University of Arts and Design, and the author of *Japanese Garden Design* and a soon-to-be-published translation of the *Sakuteiki,* Japan's 1,000-year-old gardening treatise. Examples of Keane's work can be found at http://www.mpkeane.com.

DOUGLAS M. ROTH is America's leading authority on Japanese pruning techniques. He lived in the Kamakura area for ten years and trained as a gardener there. Now he publishes *The Journal of Japanese Gardening*, and designs and maintains Japanese gardens in the northeastern United States. His company, ROTH Tei-en, hosts regular pruning and stone-setting workshops. They also sponsor a two-week garden study tour to Kyoto each year.

DAVID SLAWSON is one of the most sought-after designers of public and private Japanese gardens in the United States. His *Secret Teachings in the Art of Japanese Gardens* is one of the most influential books on the subject. He lives in Cleveland, Ohio.

ILLUSTRATIONS AND PHOTOS
Illustrations by **STEVE BUCHANAN**
DENCY KANE cover (garden designed by Julie Moir Messervy), 19, 27, 35, 36, 39, 45, 67, 71 left, 95 left, 97
REX A. BUTCHER pages 1, 6, 8
CHARLES MANN pages 5, 20, 26, 29, 38, 50
JOHN GLOVER pages 7, 53, 60, 73, 80, 84, 88, 95 right
DAVID SLAWSON pages 11, 16, 18, 22, 43, 55
MARGE GARFIELD pages 12, 30, 70
JERRY PAVIA pages 13, 14, 15, 31 right, 37, 42, 46, 47, 75, 78 left, 81, 85, 86
DAVID CAVAGNARO pages 21, 40, 51, 72, 76, 82 left and right, 91, 93, 98 top
SYLVIA M. BANKS page 23
DAVID ENGEL pages 25, 31 left, 32 top and bottom, 41, 52
DEREK FELL pages 33, 56
JUDY GLATTSTEIN page 49
JOSEPH DE SCIOSE page 59
ALAN & LINDA DETRICK pages 69, 71 right, 74, 78 right, 94 left and right
SUSAN M. GLASCOCK pages 79, 89, 90, 98 bottom

INDEX

A

Acer, 83
  capillipes, 74
  circinatum, 73
  griseum, 74
  japonicum, 73
  palmatum, 72-73
  pensylvanicum, 47, 73-74
  rufinerve, 74
  spicatum, 73
Ackerman, William, 89
Acorus, 52, 87
Actaea
  alba, 75
  asiatica, 75
  pachypoda, 75
  rubra, 75
Adiantum pedatum, 46
Amelanchier, 21, 83, 77, 87
Anise, Purple, 87
Apricot, Japanese, 67, 74-75
Arborvitae, 77
Arctostaphylos
  alpina, 92
  edmundsii, 92
  hookeri, 92
  nevadensis, 92
  nummularia, 92
  uva-ursi, 91-92
Arisaema, 51, 87
Arrow wood, 87, 91
Asarum
  blumei, 76
  canadense, 76, 87
  caudatum, 76
  europaeum, 75
  nipponicum, 76
  shuttleworthii, 75-76
  takaoi, 75
Ash, American Mountain, 68
Ashikaga Yoshimasa, 11
Aster, 83, 92
Athyrium
  filix-femina, 98
  niponicum, 98
Azalea, 58, 71-72

B

Balance, in pruning, 64-65
Balloon Flower, 83, 87
Bamboo, 93, 94-95
Baneberry, 75
Barberry, Japanese, 68
Bayberry, 90-91
Bearberry, 91-92
Berberis thunbergii, 68
Blueberry, 83, 87, 92
Boxwood, 58
Bulbs, suppliers of, 102-103
Bushclover, 80-81, 92

C

Camellia, 77
  japonica, 88, 89
  oleifera, 89
  sasanqua (sazanka), 88-89
  sinensis (tea), 88
Camphor Tree, 68
Carex
  dolichostachya, 94
  oshimensis, 94
  pensylvanica, 94
  plantaginea, 94
Carpinus caroliniana, 87
Cedar
  Japanese/Yakushima, 69-70
Cercis, 77
Chamaecyparis
  lawsoniana, 69
  nootkatensis, 69
  obtusa, 69
  pisifera, 69
  thyoides, 69
Chionanthus
  retusus, 77, 80, 87
  virginicus, 77, 79-80, 87
Chrysopsis mariana, 92
Cinnamomum camphora, 68
City gardens, 45-48
Clethra

  acuminata, 77, 84
  alnifolia, 84-85, 92
  barbinervis, 77, 85
Conder, Josiah, 12, 15
Container water gardens, 47-48
Cornus florida, 68, 73
Courtyard gardens, 5, 12, 46
Crabapple, 83
Cryptomeria japonica, 21, 69-70
Cypress
  Bald, 87
  False, 69

D

Daisen-in, 9, 10, 11, 18
Darmera peltata, 51-52, 87
Design, 9-23
  dry gardens, 10-11, 21, 34, 41, 44, 52-53
  formulaic, 5, 9-10, 11-13, 33, 43, 44
  information sources, 104-105
  integration, 5-6, 22-23
  local materials in, 10, 14, 16, 20, 46
  natural habitat principle of, 7, 20-23, 67-68
  planes, 18
  proportional relationships in, 17
  public gardens, 44-45
  S-curve/Z-zigzag, 19-20
  stroll gardens, 28-30
  tea gardens, 11, 13, 24-28, 31, 44
  user/site considerations in, 10, 13-14, 16
  See also Paths; Rocks; Stones/stone artifacts; Water gardens
Diagonal plane, 18
Dianthus superbus, 81

Dicranum
  flagellare, 97
  scoparium, 97
Dirr, Michael, 73
Disporum, 77
Dogwood, 68, 73
Dry gardens, 10-11, 21, 34, 41, 44, 52-53
Dryopteris, 98

E
Engel, David, 6, 10, 34-43
Epimedium
  grandiflorum, 77, 83
  sempervirens, 77, 83
Equisetum telmateia, 48
Erythronium americanum, 87
Eupatorium chinense, 81

F
Farfugium japonicum, 86, 92
Fences, backdrop for, 46, 48
Fern, 45-46, 75, 76, 96, 98
  Buckler, 98
  Christmas, 46
  Cinnamon, 98
  Japanese Painted, 98
  Lady, 98
  Maidenhair, 46
  New York, 98
  Ostrich, 98
  Royal, 98
  suppliers, 102
Foamflower, 77
Franklinia alatamaha, 89
Fringe Tree, 77, 79-80, 87
Furuta Oribe, 11

G
Gate, middle, 27
Ginger, Wild, 75-76, 87
Glattstein, Judy, 6, 44-53
Grapeholly, 70-71
Grasses, 93-94, 103

H
Hakonechloa, 82
Halesia, 77, 83, 87
Hamamelis, 80, 87
  japonica, 77, 80

mollis, 77, 80
virginiana, 77, 80
Hemlock
  Eastern, 21, 68
Herbaceous plants
  hills/fields, 80-83
  mountain/forest, 75-76, 77
  ponds/streams, 51-52, 86-87
  seashore, 91-92
  suppliers, 100-102
Hills and fields
  herbaceous plants, 80-83
  trees and shrubs, 78-80, 83
Holly
  American, 21, 90
  Japanese, 77, 84
Horizontal plane, 18
Hornbeam, 77, 87
Horsetail, giant, 48
Hosta, 83
Human scale, 57-58
Hypnum imponens, 97-98

I
Ilex
  crenata, 77, 84
  glabra, 84, 92
  opaca, 90
Illicium floridanum, 87
Illustrations for Designing Mountain, Water, and Hillside Field Landscapes, 15, 16, 17, 18, 22, 67, 68
Imperata cylindrica, 93
Inkberry, 84, 92
Invasive plants, 68, 93-95
Iris
  Blue Flag (*versicolor*), 52, 87
  Japanese Water (*ensata*), 87
Itoh, Teiji, 11

J
Jack-in-the-pulpit, 51, 87
Japanese Garden Construction (Newsom), 14
Jonas, Patricia, 4-7, 66-98

Juniperus (Juniper)
  chinensis, 90
  communis, 83, 90
  procumbens, 90
  virginiana, 83

K
Kalmia latifolia, 47, 70
Karesansui
  See Dry gardens
Katsura Imperial Villa and Garden, Kyoto, 5
Keane, Marc Peter, 6, 24-33
Kobori Enshu, 13-14
Kuck, Loraine, 12
Kuo Hsi, 9

L
Landscape Architecture in Japan (Conder), 12
Lespedeza, 80-81
  bicolor, 81
  capitata, 81, 92
  cuneata, 81
  intermedia, 92
  thunbergii, 81
Leucothoe, 77
Lilium
  auratum, 81-82
  pardalinum, 83
  philadelphicum, 82, 92
  speciosum, 82
  superbum, 82-83
Lily, 81-83
  Leopard, 83
  Meadow, 83
  Trout, 87
  Turk's Cap, 82-83
  Wood, 82, 92
Lindera
  benzoin, 85
  obtusiloba, 77, 85
  umbellata, 85-86
Liriope, 82

M
Mahonia, 70-71
Malus, 83
Maple, 67, 72-74, 83
  Full-moon, 73
  Japanese, 72-73
  Mountain, 21, 73

Paperbark, 74
Redvein, 74
Snakebark, 74
Striped-bark, 47, 73-74
Vine, 73
Matteuccia struthiopteris, 98
Merry-bells, 76, 77
Miscanthus sinensis, 81, 94
Mitchella, 83
  repens, 76, 79
  undulata, 76
Mosses
  care of, 46, 96
  establishing, 96-97
  recommended species, 97-98
  on rocks, 46
  suppliers, 103
Moss Temple (Saiho-ji), 96
Mountain and forest
  herbaceous plants, 75-76, 77
  trees and shrubs, 69-75, 77
Mountain Laurel, 47, 70
Muhlenbergia, 94
Muso Soseki, 96
Myrica pensylvanica, 90-91

N
Nakane, Kinsaku, 10, 21
Nandina domestica, 93
Native plants, 21-22, 47
Natural habitat principle, 7, 21-23, 67-68
Newsom, Samuel, 14
Nobedan, 31-32

O
Ophiopogon, 82
Osmanthus, 87
Osmunda
  cinnamomea, 98
  japonica, 98
  regalis, 98
Ostrya, 77, 87

P
Partridgeberry, 76, 79, 83
Paths
  asymmetrical design, 32-33
  materials, 30-31, 32

nobedan, 31-32
punctuation stones, 32
S-curve, 19, 46
stepping stones, 11-12, 13, 20, 31, 32, 40-41, 46
stroll garden, 28-30
tea garden, 24-28, 31
Patrinia
  scabiosifolia, 81
  villosa, 83
Peaks, rock, 39-40
Pepperbush
  Japanese, 77, 85
  Mountain, 77, 84
  Sweet, 84-85, 92
Persimmon, 20
Phyllostachys, 95
Pine
  Black, 60, 67, 78
  Eastern White, 77, 78-79
  Lacebark, 77, 78-79
  Pitch, 79
  Ponderosa, 77, 78
  pruning of, 60-61
  Red, 78
  Scots, 60, 77, 78-79
  Shore, 60, 79
Pinus
  bungeana, 77, 78-79
  contorta, 60, 79, 92
  densiflora, 78
  ponderosa, 77, 78
  rigida, 79, 92
  strobus, 77, 78-79
  sylvestris, 60, 77, 78-79
  thunbergii, 60, 67, 78, 92
Platycodon grandiflorus, 81, 83, 87
Pleioblastus, 95
Polygonatum
  biflorum, 86
  humile, 87
  lasianthum, 87
  odoratum, 86-87
Polystichum acrostichoides, 46
Polytrichum
  commune, 96, 98
  juniperinum, 98
  piliferum, 98
Ponds and streams
  artificial, 50-51

herbaceous plants, 51-52, 86-87
natural water garden, 49-50
  rocks in, 41, 42
  trees and shrubs, 84-86, 87
Proportion, in design, 17-18
Pruning, 13, 54-65, 66, 78-79
  for aesthetic effect, 56-57
  emulation of nature, 54, 56
  to human scale, 57-58
  natural balance principle in, 64-65
  S-curve/Z-zigzag, 20
  shrub shapes, 58-59
  for space constraint, 58
  techniques of, 61-64
  tools for, 61
  tree shapes, 59-61
Prunus, 77
  maritima, 92
  mume, 67, 74-75
Pseudosasa japonica, 95
Public gardens, 44-45
Pueraria lobata, 81

R
Raked gravel, 44, 52
Redbud, 77
Retaining walls, 39
Rhododendron
  calendulaceum, 72
  degronianum, 69, 71
  indicum, 71
  kaempferi, 71
  periclymenoides, 71-72
Rikyu, *See* Sen no Rikyu, 11, 22-23
Rocks, 34-43
  mossy, 46
  in naturalistic landscape, 36-37
  peaks, 39-40
  placement of, 37-38, 45-46
  at pond edges, 41
  retaining walls, 39
  in seashore landscape, 41
  stepping stones, 11-12, 13, 20, 31, 32, 40-41, 46
  in streams, 42

symbolic role of, 34-35
utilitarian use of, 35
in waterfall construction, 42-43
in Zen temple gardens, 34
See also Stones/stone artifacts
Roth, Douglas, 6, 54-65
Ryoan-ji, 11

S
Saiho-ji, 96
Sakuteiki, 20-21, 30
Sandberry, 91-92
Sano, Tansai, 10
Sasaella ramosa, 95
Sasa palmata, 95
Sassafras, 20, 77, 92
Sciadopitys verticillata, 72
S-curve design, 19-20, 46
Seashore
herbaceous plants, 91-92
rocks in, 41
trees and shrubs, 88-91, 92
Sedges, 93-94, 103
Senna hebecarpa, 87
Sen no Rikyu, 11, 22-23
Serviceberry, 77, 83, 87
Shibataea kumasaca, 95
Shortia, 77
Shrubs. *See* Trees and shrubs
Silverbell, 77, 83, 87
Sisyrinchium angustifolium, 87
Slawson, David, 4, 9-23, 67, 68
Smilacina, 77
Solomon's Seal, 86-87
False, 77
Sorbus americana, 68
Space and Illusion in the Japanese Garden (Teiji Itoh), 11
Spicebush, 85-86
Spiraea japonica, 68
Stepping stones, 11-12, 13, 20, 31, 32, 40-41, 46
Stewartia, 21
monadelpha, 77, 89
ovata, 77, 89-90
pseudocamellia, 77, 89

Stones/stone artifacts, 35
formulaic use of, 13
local materials, 14, 46
punctuation stones, 32
stepping stones, 11-12, 13, 20, 31, 32, 40-41, 46
suppliers, 103
water basins, 13, 14, 27, 44, 46, 47
See also Rocks
Strawbell, 87
Streams. *See* Ponds and streams
Stroll gardens, 28-30
Suppliers, 100-103
Sweet Flag, 52, 87

T
Taxodium distichum, 87
Tea gardens, 11, 13, 24-28, 31, 44
Tenshin-en, 21
Ternstroemia gymnanthera, 92
Thelypteris novaeboracensis, 98
Thuja occidentalis, 77
Tiarella, 77
Tools
pruning, 61
suppliers, 103
Trees and shrubs
height of, 57-58
hills/fields, 78-80, 83
invasive, 68
mountain/forest, 69-75, 77
native plants, 21-22, 47
ponds/streams, 84-86, 87
seashore, 88-91, 92
shape and position, 58-60
suppliers, 100-102
See also Pruning
Tsubo-niwa, *See* Courtyard Gardens
Tsukubai, *See* Water basins
Tsuga canadensis, 68
Tsukiyama Teizoden, 15

U
Umbrella Pine, 72
Umbrella Plant, 51-52, 87
Uvularia, 77, 87

V
Vaccinium, 83, 87, 92
Vertical plane, 18
Viburnum
dentatum, 83, 87, 91
prunifolium, 77
Viola pedata, 92
Violet, Bird's Foot, 92

W
Walls
backdrop for, 46, 48
retaining, 39, 50
Water basins, 13, 14, 27, 44, 47
Water drip, 47
Waterfalls, 42-43, 51
Water gardens, 45-53
for arid climates, 52-53
artificial ponds, 50-51
city yards, 45-46
container, 47-48
natural water, 48-49
spiritual connotation of, 44
See also Ponds and streams
Wisteria, 68
Witch Hazel, 77, 80, 87
World of the Japanese Garden, The (Kuck), 12

Y
Yew, 58

Z
Zen temple gardens, 34, 88
Z-zigzag design, 19-20

BROOKLYN BOTANIC GARDEN

RELATED BOOKS

FROM BBG

BROOKLYN BOTANIC GARDEN

handbooks are available at a discount

from our web site

www.bbg.org/gardenemporium

OR CALL (718) 623-7286

JOIN THE BROOKLYN BOTANIC GARDEN OR GIVE A GIFT OF MEMBERSHIP

Here are the membership benefits you can enjoy and share with others:

SUBSCRIBER $35

- Subscriptions to *21st-Century Gardening Series* handbooks and *Plants & Gardens News*
- Use of Gardener's Resource Center
- Reciprocal privileges at botanical gardens across the country

INDIVIDUAL $35

- One membership card for free individual admission
- 10% discount at the Garden Gift Shop
- Entry to members' summer hours, Sunset Picnics, and Preview Night at the Plant Sale
- Discounts on adult classes, trips, and tours
- *BBG Members News* and course catalog mailings
- Use of Gardener's Resource Center
- Reciprocal privileges at botanical gardens across the country

FAMILY/DUAL $65

All of the above INDIVIDUAL benefits, plus
- 2 membership cards for free admission for 2 adults & their children under 16
- Free parking for 4 visits
- 10% discount at the Terrace Cafe
- Discounts on children's programs and classes
- Subscriptions to *21st-Century Gardening Series* handbooks and *Plants & Gardens News*

FAMILY/DUAL PLUS $95

All of the above, plus
- 1 guest admitted free each time you come
- Free parking for 8 visits
- 2 SUBSCRIBER gift memberships for the price of one

SIGNATURE $150

All of the above, plus
- Your choice of one Signature Plant
- Free parking for 12 visits
- A special BBG gift calendar

SPONSOR $300

All of the above, plus
- Your choice of 2 Signature Plants
- 4 complimentary one-time guest passes
- Free parking for 18 visits

PATRON $500

All of the above, plus
- 2 guests admitted free each time you come
- Recognition in selected printed materials
- Free parking for 24 visits

GAGER SOCIETY $1500

All of the above, plus
- Unlimited free guests each time you come
- Gager Society Dinner and garden trip
- Complimentary INDIVIDUAL gift membership for a friend
- Private receptions for higher level donors
- Unlimited free parking for a year

Please use the form on reverse to join.
For more information, call the Membership Department: 718-623-7210

MEMBERSHIP FORM

Your Name

Address

City   State   Zip   Membership #

Daytime phone   Evening phone

email   ☐ Check if this is a renewal.

Please enroll me as a member of the Brooklyn Botanic Garden.

☐ Subscriber $35   ☐ Signature $150
☐ Individual $35   ☐ Sponsor $300
☐ Family/Dual $65   ☐ Patron $500
☐ Family/Dual Plus $95   ☐ Gager Society $1500

Please send a gift membership to the recipient below.

☐ Subscriber $35   ☐ Signature $150
☐ Individual $35   ☐ Sponsor $300
☐ Family/Dual $65   ☐ Patron $500
☐ Family/Dual Plus $95   ☐ Gager Society $1500

Gift Recipient's Name

Address

City   State   Zip

Daytime phone   Evening phone

email

Method of Payment

☐ Check (payable to Brooklyn Botanic Garden)
☐ Visa ☐ MasterCard ☐ AMEX

Card #   Exp. Date

Signature

Please tear along perforation, complete form and return with payment to:
Membership Office, Brooklyn Botanic Garden,
1000 Washington Avenue, Brooklyn, NY 11225-1099
Phone: 718-623-7210 Fax: 718-857-2430